GRAY
MATTER

The Neurobiology
of Addiction

GRAY MATTER

GRAY
MATTER

The Neurobiology of Addiction

James D. Stoehr

Professor

Colleges of Medicine and
Health Sciences

Midwestern University

CHELSEA HOUSE
PUBLISHERS
A Haights Cross Communications Company ®
Philadelphia

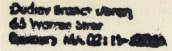

CHELSEA HOUSE PUBLISHERS

VP, NEW PRODUCT DEVELOPMENT Sally Cheney
DIRECTOR OF PRODUCTION Kim Shinners
CREATIVE MANAGER Takeshi Takahashi
MANUFACTURING MANAGER Diann Grasse
PRODUCTION EDITOR Noelle Nardone
PHOTO EDITOR Sarah Bloom

STAFF FOR THE NEUROBIOLOGY OF ADDICTION

PROJECT MANAGEMENT Dovetail Content Solutions
DEVELOPMENTAL EDITOR Carol Field
PROJECT MANAGER Pat Mrozek
PHOTO EDITOR Robin Landry
SERIES AND COVER DESIGNER Terry Mallon
LAYOUT Maryland Composition Company, Inc.

Library of Congress Cataloging-in-Publication Data

Stoehr, James D.
    The neurobiology of addiction / James D. Stoehr.
        p. cm.—(Gray matter)
    Includes bibliographical references and index.
        ISBN 0-7910-8574-0
    1. Substance abuse—Physiological aspects. 2. Neuropsychology. 3. Brain. I. Title. II.
Series.
    RC564.S76 2005
    616.86—dc22   2005011989

YA

3/06

Contents

1 Drug and Alcohol Addiction: Overview

The human brain is capable of creating complex and beautiful things. It is capable of undying love and compassion for others and of true selflessness and generosity. However, the human brain is also capable of intolerance and cruelty, and the brain itself is not immune to its own destructive powers. The needs and wants of the human brain can overcome its abilities for reason and rational thought to the point of self-destruction and even death. This can be the case in **drug** and alcohol **addiction**.

To fully understand the problem of drug and alcohol addiction, one must appreciate the processes that occur in the human brain during the phases of **drug use, abuse, dependence**, and addiction. Fundamental to this appreciation is the concept that drug and alcohol addiction is a brain disease. Scientific evidence implicates the human brain as both the underlying cause and ultimate solution to the problem of addiction. Our brains are responsible for all of our thoughts, motivations, and actions. The human brain is susceptible to all drugs of abuse. Ultimately these drugs change the chemistry and functioning of the human brain and lead to impaired judgments and actions that can result in chronic drug use. Yet the same human brain is capable of understanding its susceptibilities, accepting its limits and, ultimately, striving for continual self-improvement and health.

The economic cost of drug and alcohol addiction is staggering. According to estimates from the National Institute on Drug Abuse (NIDA) and the National Institute on Alcohol Abuse and Alcoholism (NIAAA), the total annual economic cost of drug and alcohol abuse exceeds $250 billion. This includes the costs of the legal consequences of drug abuse (law enforcement, incarceration of prisoners, drug traffic control), lost work productivity (of both victims and perpetrators), property damage, and health-related costs (premature deaths, drug-related illnesses, and healthcare). Although some of us have not experienced these consequences first-hand, we may know someone who abuses drugs. They may smoke or drink too much, misuse prescription medications, or use **illicit** drugs occasionally. What they have in common is that they are all taking risks with their health and safety. Drug and alcohol abuse is our number one public health concern.

Nevertheless, the benefits of science-based drug education and prevention programs are beginning to be realized. Recent trends in the attitudes and behaviors of high school students indicate that, in general, drug use is on the decline by school-aged children and teenagers. Consider the following statistics from the University of Michigan's annual Monitoring the Future Survey of more than 48,000 school children from around the country in 2003:

- The use of **marijuana** and **MDMA** (Ecstasy) declined in 8th graders since 2002.
- The use of **amphetamines, tranquilizers**, and MDMA by 10th and 12th graders also declined.
- The use of heroin, crack cocaine, and steroids declined among 10th graders.
- However, **inhalant** use by 8th graders increased from the previous year, and the use of **Vicodin®** and **OxyContin®** continues to rise in all age groups.

Furthermore, consider the absolute numbers of these children who are using these drugs (when 1% roughly equals 40,000 kids nationwide):

- Within the last month 17% of these individuals used tobacco products, 33% used alcohol, 15% used marijuana, and 4% used amphetamines.
- Each day approximately 3,000 teenagers start smoking cigarettes; one third will become daily smokers.
- Peak lifetime drug use occurs in the young adult age group (ages 18–25).
- Within the last month non-medical use of prescription **painkillers** by young adults jumped by 15%.
- More than 60% of all patients who enter drug treatment programs started using drugs at age 20 or younger.

Most drug and alcohol use starts at an early age. Recent studies have also suggested that approximately a third of adolescent alcohol users will progress to alcohol abuse or dependence, and approximately half of adolescent drug users will make the transition to drug abuse or dependence. Drug and alcohol use typically starts as an experiment. Curiosity and peer pressure may be significant factors during this stage. **Recreational** or **social** use may follow as the user increases the frequency of drug or alcohol use. As the user starts to become adapted to the drug, more (larger doses) will be required to achieve the same feeling or effect (**tolerance**). At this point, drug abuse can rapidly progress to addiction (**compulsive** drug use despite harmful consequences). See Table 1.1 for typical signs and symptoms of drug or alcohol addiction.

Addiction is chronic (persistent and long lasting), progressive (increasing in severity), and characterized by **relapse** (regression or transition into worsening state following partial recovery). The pace with which abusers may progress through these stages

Table 1.1 Signs and Symptoms of Drug Dependence and Addiction

1 Loss of natural rewards	Previously important social or recreational activities reduced
2 Escalation	Drug is taken in larger amounts for longer periods of time
3 Uncontrolled use	Unsuccessful attempts to cut down
4 Time devoted to drug	A lot of time spent on getting drug, using drug, or recovering from drug use
5 Tolerance	Using more to achieve same effect; using same amount and getting reduced effect
6 **Withdrawal**	Characteristic drug withdrawal syndromes (most often opposite symptoms to that of drug's effects)
7 Continued harm	Drug use despite knowing that physical or psychological harm is being done

From Diagnostic and Statistical Manual of Mental Disorders, 4th Edition, and Principles of Addiction Medicine, 3rd Edition.

depends on several factors, including their genetic **predisposition** (addiction that runs in their family), their social **context** (amount of stress or anxiety in their lives), and the drug in question (some drugs are more addicting or potent than others). It is important to understand that drug and alcohol addiction is treatable. Addicted individuals should be treated without judgment or stereotypes and will need the support of family, friends, employers, and health care providers in order to remain drug free and healthy.

Is drug addiction a brain disease or a matter of choice? Is it determined by the genes you've inherited or is it determined by the environment in which you were raised? Why can't drug users just simply stop? Is there something wrong with their brains? What happens inside the brains of drug users? Answers to these and other questions concerning drug abuse are being studied and investigated by counselors, clinicians, teachers, and scientists. In this book we will examine recent scientific evidence that implicates addiction as a brain disease. We will look at images of a brain that is damaged by drug use, a brain that is craving cocaine, and the genetics of alcoholism. We will consider what happens in the human brain as users progress from casual drug use to abuse and addiction, and then discuss how the brain recovers after addiction.

■ **Learn more about addiction** Search the Internet for *teen drug use*, *drug addiction defined*, or *signs of drug addiction*.

SUMMARY POINTS

- Drug and alcohol addiction is a chronic and progressive brain disease.
- Addiction is influenced by genetics, environment, and drug use.
- Overall rates of drug use by teenagers has declined in recent years.
- Abuse of inhalants and prescription painkillers is on the rise.
- Addiction is characterized by loss of control, use despite harm, tolerance, withdrawal, and denial.

2 | The Brain and Our Behavior

How drugs affect the human brain determines how they affect human behavior. All drugs of abuse alter specific brain chemicals located in different areas of the brain. These areas are also responsible for different functions.

BRAIN STRUCTURE AND FUNCTIONS

One area of the brain may be generally responsible for vision, or hearing, or controlling muscle movement, or thinking and reasoning. The more complex functions of the brain, such as decision making, planning, language, and sensory processing, are located in the outer surface called the **cerebral cortex** (Figure 2.1). The cerebral cortex is sensitive to the immediate, intoxicating effects of drugs as well as the long-term effects and damage that drugs can cause.

The **limbic system**, located below the cerebral cortex, is responsible for emotions and some forms of **short-term memory**. The limbic system is particularly sensitive to drugs of abuse, which alter our emotions and the way we feel. It is made up of several interconnected structures including the **hippocampus** (involved with learning and memory), the **amygdala** (responsible for negative emotions such as fear and aggression), certain parts of the **thalamus** (responsible for relaying sensory information to the cerebral cortex and limbic structures), and the **hy-**

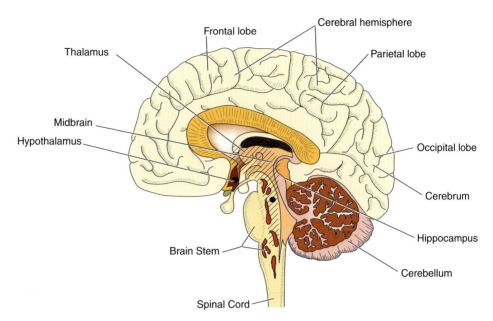

Figure 2.1 Different structures of the brain are responsible for different functions. This diagram shows the locations of important structures that are affected by drugs of abuse.

pothalamus (which controls body temperature, hunger, thirst, sleep cycles, and the physical responses to emotional situations). All of these areas are susceptible to particular drugs of abuse. Some drugs decrease appetite (the effect of **amphetamines** in the hypothalamus), some cause short-term memory problems and "**black-outs**" (the effect of alcohol in the hippocampus), and some may increase aggression (long-term effect of steroid abuse on the amygdala).

Located below the limbic system is the **midbrain** (Figure 2.2). The midbrain contains groups of cells (known as **nuclei**) that produce brain chemicals called **neurotransmitters** that are distributed throughout other areas of the brain. These will be discussed in more detail in Chapter 3. These nuclei can be considered the chemical manufacturing plants in the brain. All drugs

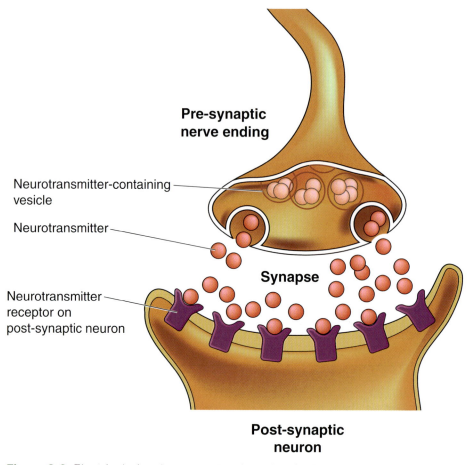

Pre-synaptic nerve ending

Neurotransmitter-containing vesicle

Neurotransmitter

Synapse

Neurotransmitter receptor on post-synaptic neuron

Post-synaptic neuron

Figure 2.2 Electrical signals are sent using chemicals called neurotransmitters. Neurotransmitters are released into the synapse, where they make contact with special receptors on the neighboring neuron.

of abuse influence the production, release, or elimination of these neurotransmitters. In addition to the nuclei that produce neurotransmitters, the midbrain also contains the **reticular activating system** (**RAS**). The RAS is responsible for many functions including regulation of sleep cycles and consciousness. The RAS is like a network of highways that transfers information from the spinal cord and the body to higher centers in the brain such as the cerebral cortex and limbic system.

The RAS is also located in the **brain stem**—the area just above the spinal cord. The brain stem also contains nuclei that are responsible for vital brain functions that are considered automatic, those that can be done without conscious effort. These functions include chewing, swallowing, vomiting, sneezing, coughing, breathing, and regulation of heart rate. An overdose of certain drugs, such as depressants, can cause death because of their affects on brain stem function (see "Binge Drinking and Alcohol Poisoning" box).

■ **Learn more about general brain functions** *Search* the Internet for *limbic system*, *prefrontal cortex*, or *reticular activating system*.

FUNCTION OF BRAIN CELLS

Brain cells, known as **neurons**, are the smallest functional unit in the central nervous system. There are over 100 billion neurons in the human brain. The function of a neuron is determined by its location within the brain and the connections it makes with other brain cells. Within a neuron, information flows in one direction from one end of the cell to the other. Signals from other cells enter a neuron in its **dendrites** and are added together at the level of the cell body (**soma**). The cell may then communicate with other cells by sending a signal (**action potential**) down its axon to the terminal endings (Figure 2.3).

Neurons do not make physical contact with one another to communicate. They are separated by gaps called **synapses**. Brain cells communicate through electrochemical signals. When an electrical signal (action potential) travels down a neuron's axon, neurotransmitters are released into the synapse. Electrical signals traveling in dendrites and axons are converted into chemical signals released into the synapse. The released neurotransmitter diffuses across the synapse very quickly and contacts the neighboring (post-synaptic) neuron. The post-synaptic cell will respond to the neurotransmitter if it expresses **receptors** on its cell surface specific for this neurotransmitter. Receptors are small proteins that recognize specific neurotransmitters. These receptors lock onto the neurotransmitter in a process called **receptor binding**, and subsequently cause an electrical change

Binge Drinking and Alcohol Poisoning

One popular method of drinking alcohol is "chugging" or gulping large amounts of alcohol in a very short period of time. Some teenagers have overdosed on alcohol (alcohol poisoning) from this drinking pattern. When individuals chug large amounts of high proof alcohol, they can ingest half of a fifth or more of liquor in the time span of a few minutes. Alcohol is absorbed quickly through the stomach and intestines, and if a high dose is consumed an individual can rapidly progress from a state of relaxation to unconsciousness in a matter of minutes. One of the brain's defense mechanisms for removing poisons in the body is to initiate vomiting (which is controlled by areas in the brain stem). If an individual loses consciousness too quickly and anesthetizes these brain stem areas that control vomiting, he or she may pass out and continue to absorb the alcohol that remains in the stomach. As the absorption of alcohol continues, the brain is further sedated and the individiual may reach a comatose state or death from respiratory or circulatory collapse very quickly. If an individual is intoxicated prior to drinking heavily or has used other depressants such as sedative-hypnotics or barbiturates, the likelihood of death increases significantly. Individuals in this condition must receive medical treatment as soon as possible. The legal limit of blood alcohol concentration (BAC) in most states is 0.08% alcohol by volume. Death occurs at a BAC of 0.50 or more. Chugging high amounts of alcohol can rapidly increase BAC from zero to 0.40 or more in a matter of less than an hour.

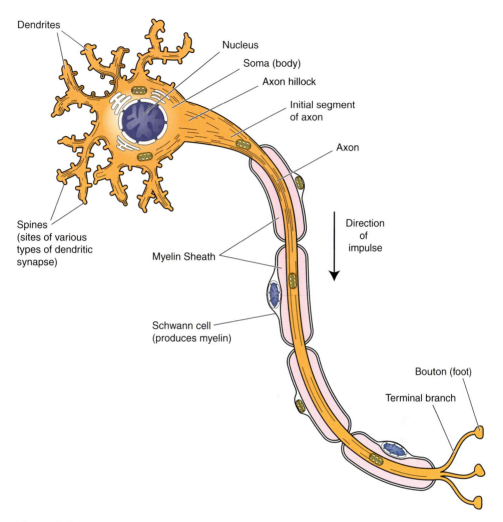

Figure 2.3 The brain has billions of cells called neurons. Each neuron, like the one shown here, has an axon that transmits information to other cells. Impulses flow in one direction, from the dendrites to the terminal branch.

known as a potential in the post-synaptic cell. A common analogy is that of a key and lock. A neurotransmitter may act as a key that fits into a specific lock (the receptor), which then permits the turning of the lock and opening of the door (post-synaptic potential). In this way, a chemical signal in the synapse is transformed into an electrical signal in the post-synaptic cell.

Each neuron may synapse with 10,000 other neurons. Billions of neurons, each connecting to thousands of other cells, permit a tremendous amount of information to be processed in the brain. Electrochemical signaling occurs very quickly in the brain. Each cell is capable of responding to thousands of neurons simultaneously. Some estimates have suggested that the human brain can process 100 trillion calculations per second with a capacity of 100 trillion bytes of memory. Even the fastest supercomputers cannot do this. The human brain not only processes information quickly, but it learns, adapts, creates, and thinks all while being light and portable.

BRAIN SYSTEMS AND BEHAVIOR

Although the integration of information may occur at the level of the synapse, complex functions of the human brain occur in larger areas in the cerebral cortex. In general, anterior (more forward) areas of the cortex are involved with planning and movement, while posterior (near the back) cortical areas are involved with the processing of **sensory** information. The cerebral cortex is further divided into the **frontal lobe, parietal lobe, temporal lobe**, and **occipital lobe**. (See Table 2.1 for a description of the general functions of each lobe and other brain regions.)

The most anterior area of the frontal lobes is known as the **pre-frontal cortex** (the area just behind your forehead). Humans possess the most developed pre-frontal cortex of all animals. Some other animals, such as chimpanzees, gorillas, dolphins, and whales are considered intelligent because they communicate and have social hierarchies. However, they do not possess large or well developed pre-frontal cortexes. This highly developed cortical area provides humans with the ability to plan for events well into the future. Most animals react on instinct or respond

Table 2.1 Brain Areas and Functions

Frontal lobe	Decision-making, reasoning, planning, behavioral inhibition, and personality
Parietal lobe	Sensation and perception of certain senses including touch
Occipital lobe	Sensation and perception of visual information
Temporal lobe	Sensation and perception of auditory information; language comprehension
Limbic system	Emotions, learning and memory, motivation
Hypothalamus	Maintains homeostasis (body temperature, eating, drinking, sleep, metabolism)
Midbrain	Neurotransmitter production
Brainstem	Vital body functions (breathing, regulation of heart rate, consciousness)
Cerebellum	Motor coordination and balance, motor learning

to stimuli, but they plan future actions very poorly. Humans can plan for years in advance, such as planning for college or a career in a certain field.

The frontal cortex also gives us personality. Human personalities can be quite varied and different from one person to another. For example, we all have different likes and dislikes, such as hobbies, different senses of humor (sarcastic versus storytelling style), and different preferences, such as tastes in art or music. The frontal lobes are also responsible for some forms of **behavioral inhibition.** In other words, certain areas in the frontal cortex are responsible for making decisions and acting appropriately based on those decisions. We all know the difference between what is right and wrong, and we all try not to make the wrong decisions. Knowing that difference and choosing the right decisions based on that knowledge are functions of the frontal lobe.

Unfortunately, the frontal lobes are particularly sensitive to long-term drug abuse and addiction. The cortical areas in the frontal lobes may become dysfunctional following chronic drug use. When this occurs, the individual's personality may change. They are not the person you once knew; they don't care about the future; they become **impulsive** and are driven to get their drug of choice and immediate gratification. They don't care about social rules and the difference between right and wrong; they become ill-mannered and may even commit crimes to support their drug habit. In this regard, addiction can be considered dehumanizing. (See "The Infamous Case of Phineas Gage" box.)

Certain areas of the cerebral cortex, including the frontal cortex, normally suppress certain thoughts, actions, and feelings. The areas of the brain responsible for expressing our emotions and organizing our movements include areas that lie underneath the cerebral cortex. These areas are continually suppressed by the cerebral cortex. Thought disorders such as **schizophrenia**, mood disorders such as **depression**, and hyperactivity disorders may occur when these sub-cortical areas are not suppressed by the cerebral cortex. Prescription amphetamines are one class of medication that is successful in the treatment of hyperactivity disorders. Ritalin® is an amphetamine-like medication that is approved for the treatment of diagnosed and documented attention deficit disorder (ADD). It seems counterintuitive for someone who is hyperactive to take a stimulant such as Ritalin. One theory is that the cerebral cortex is not effective in turning off sub-cortical **motor** areas in the brains of individuals with ADD. Ritalin® stimulates their cerebral cortex, which in turn can effectively inhibit the underlying motor control areas, thereby allowing the individual to remain calm and focused. However, these medications must be taken in strict accordance with the clinician's orders to be effective.

The human brain is composed of two sides, the left and right **hemispheres**, which continuously communicate and share information with each other. Most functions of the cerebral cortex are found on both hemispheres of the human brain. In

The Infamous Case of Phineas Gage

Phineas Gage was a mid-19th century railroad worker from Vermont. In 1848, while preparing a powder charge in a hole with a tamping iron, the charge exploded and sent the tamping iron (which was 2.5-cm in diameter) through his left cheek, left eye, and the frontal lobes of his brain. After months of recovering from his injuries, his personality was remarkably different than before the accident. His friends even said, "Gage was no longer Gage." Prior to the accident, Phineas was a well-mannered, calm, and responsible worker. Following the accident, he was anti-social, ill-mannered, self-centered, told lies constantly, and could no longer hold his job or plan for his future. His physician at the time wrote that "the equilibrium between his intellectual faculties and animal propensities seems to have been destroyed." Today we know that Phineas suffered damage to his prefrontal cortex (a brain area responsible for emotional control, decision-making, planning, and inhibition of drives). Other patients with prefrontal cortex damage have been reported to exhibit the same change in behavioral control. Drug-addicted individuals also experience the same behavioral changes (drives toward immediate gratifications, loss of long-term planning, selfishness, and lack of regard for social rules). In this regard, the prefrontal cortex of the addicted brain is unable to control behavior including the continued self-administration of drugs.

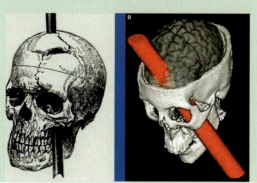

other words, both halves of the occipital lobe in the back of the brain are responsible for vision, both halves of the temporal lobes are responsible for hearing, and both halves of the frontal cortex are responsible for planning and decision making. However, there is one function that is typically unilateral and found on one hemisphere—language—which is most often located on the left hemisphere.

Human language is separated in the brain into areas for comprehension and speech. Wernicke's area is responsible for making sense of words that we hear or read, while Broca's area is responsible for organizing the necessary muscular activities required for speech, such as controlling our lips, tongue, and breathing so that we can make sounds. These areas require a significant blood supply so that oxygen is constantly delivered. This blood supply may be disrupted during periods of very high blood pressure that may occur with drug use. Several cases of strokes in young people have been caused by cocaine or amphetamine overdose. **Strokes** occur when a blood vessel ruptures or is blocked in or around the brain, causing disruption of the blood and oxygen supply to the brain. If the language areas of the brain are affected, the individual may lose the ability to understand language (Wernicke's **aphasia**) or the ability to speak (Broca's aphasia) or both (global aphasia). If the person is fortunate, the right side of the brain may start understanding language or start speaking. However, the lost functions may take several years to fully return, if they return at all.

■ **Learn more about the function of brain cells** Search the Internet for *neurons, receptor theory,* or *drug abuse and frontal cortex.*

SUMMARY POINTS

- The cerebral cortex is responsible for complex functions such as reasoning, thinking, and planning.
- Our emotions and memories are processed in an area of the brain under the cortex in the limbic system.
- The midbrain produces brain chemicals called neurotransmitters.
- Vital functions of the brain, such as controlling breathing and heart rate, are located in the brain stem.
- The vast number of synapses in the brain allow enormous amounts of information to be processed.
- The synapse is a favorite target for drugs of abuse.
- The frontal cortex is important for planning, decision making, impulse control, and personality.

Brain Regions Involved in Addiction

In the last chapter, we described how the brain's ability to complete complex tasks is due to the enormous amount of information integrated in trillions of synapses in the central nervous system. All addictive drugs affect synaptic transmission, neurotransmitters, or receptor systems in the brain, which will ultimately determine the feelings, thoughts, or actions of the drug user. In this chapter we will review the specific neurotransmitters and brain areas that are affected by all drugs of abuse.

THE MAJOR NEUROTRANSMITTER SYSTEMS IMPLICATED IN ADDICTION

To be considered a neurotransmitter, a chemical must be synthesized in a neuron, released into a synapse, affect a post-synaptic neuron or organ, and be inactivated by specific mechanisms. There are two main classes of neurotransmitters: small molecule transmitters and **neuropeptides** (Table 3.1). Neuropeptides are short chains of amino acids synthesized from proteins within cells. Small molecule transmitters are synthesized in the neurons from dietary amino acids. These neurotransmitters are used in the brain, spinal cord, and nerves that are distributed throughout the body. We will discuss the four small molecule transmitters that are most of-

Table 3.1 Major Neurotransmitter Systems Implicated in Addiction and Their Common Functions

NEURO TRANSMITTER	SITE OF PRODUCTION	TARGETS	COMMON FUNCTIONS
Serotonin (5-HT)	Dorsal raphe nuclei in brain stem	Widely distributed (forebrain, midbrain)	Regulation of sleep and mood
Norepinephrine (NE)	Locus ceruleus in brain stem	Widely distributed	Arousal, alertness
Dopamine (DA)	Midbrain	Striatum, limbic system, cerebral cortex	Movement, pleasure
GABA	Distributed throughout brain in interneurons	Neighboring neurons	Major inhibitory neurotransmitter
Opioid neuropeptides	Midbrain	Midbrain, limbic system	Decrease pain signals, behavioral reinforcement

ten affected by drugs of abuse: **serotonin, norepinephrine, dopamine,** and **gamma-aminobutyric acid.**

Serotonin

Serotonin (5-hydroxytryptamine or 5-HT) is synthesized from dietary tryptophan in large cells located in distributed brain stem nuclei called the **dorsal raphe system** (Figure 3.1). The dorsal raphe nuclei project their axons throughout the brain and spinal cord, including higher centers in the limbic system and cerebral cortex. A single dorsal raphe cell may project to hundreds of cells that are widely distributed throughout the brain. The effects of serotonin on complex neural systems and human behavior depend on the target site of serotonin's actions. For instance, serotonin released into the **pons** and midbrain controls sleep cycles, including rapid eye movement (**REM**) **sleep**. The visual images that occur during dreaming in REM sleep are

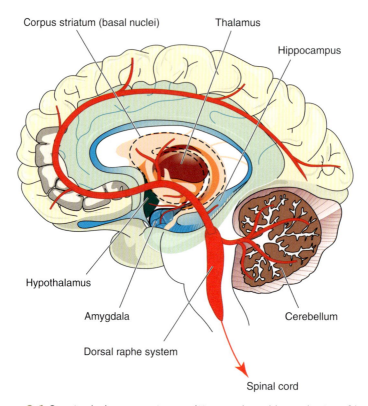

Corpus striatum (basal nuclei)   Thalamus

Hippocampus

Hypothalamus

Amygdala   Cerebellum

Dorsal raphe system

Spinal cord

Figure 3.1 Serotonin is a neurotransmitter produced by a cluster of brain stem nuclei called the dorsal raphe system (red in this figure). Neurons in the dorsal raphe system project axons throughout the brain. The effect of serotonin depends upon the brain system into which it is released.

thought to be due to inactivation of specific serotonin cells in the brain stem. Lysergic acid diethylamide (**LSD**) is thought to cause visual hallucinations because of its inhibition of these same serotonin cells in the brain stem.

Serotonin has also been implicated in such mood disorders as depression. Medications called specific serotonin reuptake inhibitors (**SSRIs**), such as Prozac® and Zoloft®, increase serotonin levels in synapses by inhibiting the **re-uptake** of serotonin by pre-synaptic raphe neurons that terminate in the limbic system and cortex. Symptoms associated with depression are relieved by the continuous elevation of serotonin levels in these synapses, which is achieved through months of treatment with these medications. However, if a specific drug of abuse is taken and a sudden release of a large amount of serotonin occurs, then rebound depression may occur when that drug is eliminated and serotonin levels fall back to normal. This is the case with use of Ecstasy (MDMA). Rebound sadness and depression following the use of MDMA is a trigger for continual administration of the drug, which may lead to MDMA-induced **toxicity** to serotonin cells in the dorsal raphe system.

Norepinephrine

Norepinephrine (NE) is produced in the **locus ceruleus** (LC), a group of tightly compacted cell bodies located in the brain stem. These cells synthesize NE from the essential amino acid tyrosine and send their projections throughout the brain in a wide distribution pattern similar to that of serotonin (Figure 3.2). The actions of NE depend upon the particular brain region into which it is released. For instance, NE released into the lateral hypothalamus can decrease appetite for food. Amphetamines that cause a large release of NE in the hypothalamus greatly amplify this effect. Norepinephrine released into the cerebral cortex is responsible for alertness and **arousal**. The more NE released into the cerebral cortex, the more alert and attentive an individual becomes. The levels of NE released in the cortex from the LC mildly fluctuate throughout the day. As a result, there are periods of the day when we feel more awake and alert, while at other times of the day we are tired and sleepy. Certain drugs of abuse, such as **stimulants** or "uppers," increase alertness and arousal and cause talkativeness, restlessness, and agitation because of their action on NE systems. For example, amphetamines can cause profound insomnia and irritability because of the increased release of NE in the hypothalamus, cortex, and limbic system.

Cells located outside the central nervous system also use norepinephrine as a chemical signal. Some of these cells are nerves,

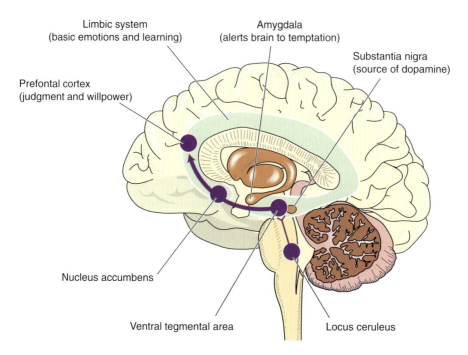

Limbic system
(basic emotions and learning)

Amygdala
(alerts brain to temptation)

Substantia nigra
(source of dopamine)

Prefontal cortex
(judgment and willpower)

Nucleus accumbens

Ventral tegmental area

Locus ceruleus

Figure 3.2 Dopamine is a neurotransmitter that is formed in several different sections of the brain. Two of these, the mesolimbic and mesocortical pathways, are located in the ventral tegmental area. Release of dopamine from the ventral tegmental area into the nucleus accumbens causes feelings of pleasure. Another dopamine production area, the substantia nigra, is slowly destroyed in patients with Parkinson's disease.

originating in the spinal cord, that stimulate specific target organs in the body. These organs are activated by emotional states such as fear and anxiety. For instance, NE will increase heart rate, breathing, blood pressure, glucose release from the liver, sweat secretion from the palms and feet, and shunt blood from internal digestive organs to the skeletal muscles during emotional stress. In this case, NE could be considered a stress signal that prepares the body for defense or action (known as the "**fight or flight response**"). NE also prepares the brain by increasing dilation of the pupils in an attempt to gain more visual information, and activating the cerebral cortex and limbic system so that a quick assessment of the threat, a decision, and appropriate action can take place.

Dopamine

Dopamine is a small molecule neurotransmitter that is similar in structure to norepinephrine. Dopamine is made in four separate systems in the brain. One system is located between the hypothalamus and pituitary gland that regulates hormone production and secretion. The other systems are located in the midbrain region (Figure 3.2). Two of these, the **mesolimbic and mesocortical pathways** of the **ventral tegmentum**, are critical to the addictive properties of drugs of abuse These systems will be discussed in greater detail later in this chapter. The fourth system, called the **nigrostriatal system**, originates in an area in the midbrain called the substantia nigra. The nigrostriatal system releases dopamine into subcortical areas involved with the striatum, which controls muscle movement. Parkinson's disease slowly destroys the nigrostriatal system in elderly individuals (Figure 3.3). As a result, they experience shaking extremities (tremors), difficulty with initiating movements (akinesia), or slow movements (bradykinesia). The reasons for the destruction of the substantia nigra in Parkinson's disease may be due to different mechanisms that are not completely understood. Nevertheless, the fact that medications that improve dopamine production and release are effective in treating the symptoms of Parkinson's suggests that dopamine does play a role in this movement disorder.

GABA

Gamma aminobutyric acid (**GABA**) is synthesized from glutamate (an amino acid) and is found in very high concentrations throughout the brain. When released onto a cell, GABA will decrease the chance that a cell will fire an action potential, and is therefore considered an **inhibitory neurotransmitter**. GABA is not synthesized in cells found in specific nuclei in the brain stem or forebrain (unlike serotonin, norepinephrine, or acetylcholine), but is synthesized in small **interneurons** found in all gray matter throughout the brain.

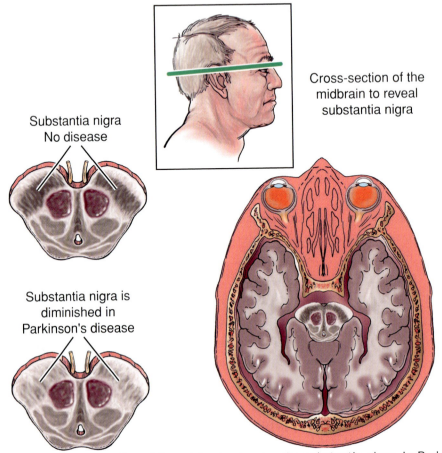

Cross-section of the midbrain to reveal substantia nigra

Substantia nigra
No disease

Substantia nigra is
diminished in
Parkinson's disease

Figure 3.3 A cross-section of the midbrain showing the substantia nigra. In Parkinson's disease, dopamine-producing neurons of the substantia nigra are lost.

Because GABA has inhibitory effects on neurons, any drug that increases the actions of GABA will decrease general brain activity and can be considered a "downer" or depressant. Depressants that act to increase GABA's actions include alcohol, sleeping pills such as Ambien, muscle relaxants such as Valium, and barbiturates such as Secobarbital. Some depressants are very powerful GABA agonists (they increase GABA activity) and cause rapid sedation, coma, and death. Drugs such as **GHB** and **Rohypnol**® are potent GABA agonists that cause a rapid loss of consciousness (suppression of cortical and NE systems) and suffocation due to respiratory failure as a result of suppression of brain stem centers that drive the diaphragm and breathing muscles in the chest.

Depressant drugs can also be considered **amnestic** agents that decrease memory formation and cause forgetfulness. Amnesia caused by depressants is due to increased GABA activity in areas normally responsible for memory formation—e.g., the cerebral cortex and hippocampus in the limbic system. Drug or alcohol "black-outs" result from suppression of activity in these brain areas. Black-outs are a symptom of increasing use and abuse of depressants, particularly alcohol, and are a warning sign of loss of control.

Depressants are also very potent when mixed with one another because they all activate the GABA systems in slightly different ways. GHB may bind the GABA receptor directly, while alcohol will bind to a different location on the receptor and magnify GHB's effect. This is why depressants are considered a class of drugs that are **synergistic** with one another. That is, the effects of two drugs mixed together might actually appear to have the effects of more than two drugs. Because of this synergistic effect, overdoses are common when different depressants are used at the same time.

NEUROPEPTIDES

Peptides are different from small molecule neurotransmitters in that they resemble proteins and are synthesized as short chains of amino acids. However, neuropeptides have actions similar to those of other neurotransmitters: they are released from neurons into synapses, have inhibitory or excitatory affects on post-synaptic neurons, and are eliminated from the synapse. Neuropeptides are often co-released into the synapse with other neurotransmitters. The actions of neuropeptides on cells are somewhat longer than that of other neurotransmitters.

Therefore, neuropeptides are often considered **neuromodulators** and influence the overall activity of networks, as well as individual, neurons.

There are several neuropeptides implicated in the behavioral effects of drugs of abuse. For instance the **opioid** family of neuropeptides is involved with the actions of opiate drugs such as heroin, morphine, OxyContin®, and other painkillers. The opioids in the human brain, such as the **endorphins** and **enkephalins**, are considered natural painkillers. These peptides surround midbrain systems involved with the transmission of sensory stimuli, especially pain sensations. These pain pathways have cells that express receptors for the opioid peptides. When opioid peptides bind these receptors, they block pain signals and there is a decreased sensation of pain. Medications that are used to control pain will also bind these receptors and decrease the transmission of pain signals to higher centers in the brain. Opioid receptors are also located on dopamine cells that are responsible for behavioral motivation and **reward**, as well the subjective sensation of **pleasure**.

■ **Learn more about brain chemicals** Search the Internet for *neurotransmitters* or *neuropeptides and addiction*.

MOTIVATION, DRIVES, AND THE CHEMISTRY OF PLEASURE

Human behavior is altered by external stimuli, such as sights and sounds in our environment, and such internal stimuli as thoughts, feelings, wants, and needs. These stimuli motivate us to act in some way or on some thing. Internal **motivation** signals tell us to act in a certain way to reach a specific goal or reward. Simple examples of motivational states include the **drives** to maintain body **homeostasis**, such as eating, drinking, regulation of body temperature, and sleep. These drives are critical for the immediate survival of an individual. When drives are not fulfilled or gratified, we feel uncomfortable and tense. We may desire the goal even more until it is satisfied and we feel subsequently relieved. Other drives include the need to reproduce and care for our offspring, which are important for survival of the species. More complex drives include personal desires such as material wealth, social stature, and power, which may not be considered critical for the survival of an individual or the species, yet may dominate the needs and wants of many individuals. Obtaining the goal or reward of the drive state can be directly pleasurable and therefore cause us to repeat that behavior when drive and desire returns. Once the reward is reached, the drive to obtain it and the motivation to act subside. In addition, the stimuli that predict the goal are ignored until the drive returns.

An example of a drive state and motivation would be the feeling of hunger. Imagine that you are late for school or work one morning and don't have time to eat breakfast. Throughout the morning you experience hunger, and your stomach may growl in anticipation of food that is overdue. Once you have time to each lunch you jump in your car to find a restaurant. On the way, you are irritable, edgy, and experience a little "road rage." The internal drive to replenish nutrients is now affecting emotional centers in your limbic system, while you ignore other cortical stimuli—your afternoon plans or traffic laws. You then begin to smell fried fast food, engaging your cerebral cortex and immediately motivating you to find the food source. You purchase and eat the fast food and are immediately gratified as your hunger drive subsides despite considerations of its nutritional value. On the way back to school or work you pass other restaurants and smell food, but you can easily ignore these aromas because the drive to eat has subsided. Drives, as we can see from this example, are very powerful motivators of human behavior.

Some drives are not the result of the absence of substances such as food in the body but are a result of external stimuli that predict reward or pleasure. Pleasure is also a powerful motivator of human behavior. The areas of the brain responsible for pleasure are believed to be the areas responsible for reinforcement. In 1954, two scientists, Olds and Milner, discovered areas in rat brains that when stimulated caused the animals to change their behavior and learn different tasks. The rats would push levers and learn to navigate mazes or other new behaviors in order to receive small electrical stimulation delivered to specific brain areas (Figures 3.4 and 3.5).

The sensitive brain areas included those that connected the midbrain and forebrain. It was later discovered that the most important brain areas for reinforcement and pleasure include the nucleus accumbens in the forebrain region. The **nucleus accumbens** (NA) receives input from dopamine-producing cells in the midbrain called the ventral tegmental area (VTA). The VTA contains dopaminergic cells that project to the frontal cortex and limbic system. Release of dopamine into the frontal cortex and nucleus accumbens result in the subjective experience of pleasure. Therefore, dopamine release causes pleasure and causes us to repeat those behaviors necessary to acquire the reward in the future. Dopamine is released when the reward is acquired (such as the tasty and gratifying fast food in our example) in addition to the presence stimuli that predict reward (such as the smell of the food that directed our behavior). In this regard, the ventral tegmental dopaminergic system is not only responsible for the pleasurable effects of natural rewards—e.g., food and artificial rewards—e.g., drugs of abuse but it also predicts expected rewards (Figure 3.6).

Addictive drugs are reinforcing. They all cause the subjective experience of pleasure and cause us to repeat drug-taking behaviors in order to re-experience the pleasure. Animals, as well as humans, will work very hard to get infusions of addictive drugs such as heroin or cocaine. The more addictive a drug is, the harder animals will work for it. They will endure painful stimuli and ignore natural rewards in order to get drugs of

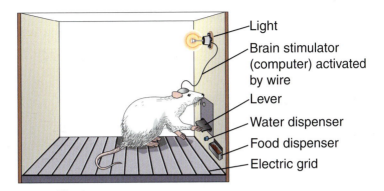

Light

Brain stimulator
(computer) activated
by wire

Lever

Water dispenser

Food dispenser

Electric grid

Figure 3.4 In 1954, the scientists James Olds and Peter Milner discovered that rats could be rewarded by stimulating specific areas in the
animals' brains. The rats would push levers or navigate mazes in order
to receive electrical stimulation to these brain areas.

abuse. Often this leads to malnourishment, dehydration, fatigue, or overdose. In all mammals, these drives to acquire the
dopamine reward can lead to failing health and even death.

If a drug activates the VTA system and increases dopamine in
the nucleus accumbens, it will cause reinforcement and addiction. However, the mechanisms of this effect and the magni-
tude of increased dopamine levels in these areas are often different. For instance, some drugs, such as the amphetamines,
increase release of dopamine from presynaptic terminals in the
nucleus accumbens. Certain drugs, such as cocaine, block the
reuptake of synaptic dopamine into the presynaptic neuron.
Other drugs of abuse, such as alcohol, act on the cell bodies in
the ventral tegmentum that produce dopamine. Addictive opiates, such as heroin and oxycodone, inhibit GABA cells that
surround and normally suppress VTA cell activity. Not all
drugs activate the dopaminergic system to the same extent and,
therefore, they possess different addictive potentials. For instance, cocaine and **methamphetamine** are much more addicting
than THC because they increase dopamine levels in the nucleus
accumbens more quickly and to a greater extent. In this regard,

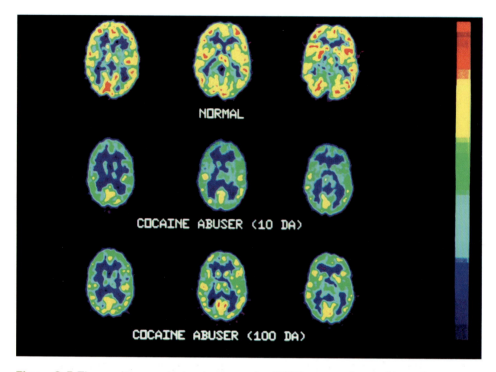

NORMAL

COCAINE ABUSER (10 DA)

COCAINE ABUSER (100 DA)

Figure 3.5 The positron emission tomography (PET) scans pictured here have been color-coded to show brain metabolism and the effects of cocaine use. Each brain scan is axial (horizontal), with the front of the brain at top. The three scans show a normal, cocaine-free brain (top), the brain of a cocaine user ten days after the last cocaine dose (middle), and 100 days after the last dose (bottom). Metabolism ranges are depicted in color, from low (dark to light blue) to high (yellow to red). The scans show the long-term recovery period, as well as the poor recovery of the front of the brain after cocaine use.

the most addictive substances are cocaine, particularly smokable crack cocaine, amphetamines (especially methamphetamine), the opiates such as heroin, morphine, and painkillers, and nicotine, which is perhaps the most addictive psychoactive drug. Other drugs of abuse, such as alcohol, Ecstasy, **Ketamine**, and prescription depressants among others, possess slightly fewer addictive properties but can also lead to similar self-destructive behaviors and addiction.

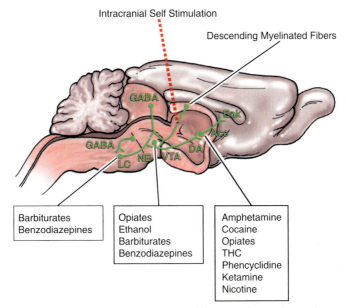

Intracranial Self Stimulation

Descending Myelinated Fibers

GABA

Enk

GABA

Acc

LC

NE

VTA

DA

Barbiturates	Opiates	Amphetamine
Benzodiazepines	Ethanol	Cocaine
	Barbiturates	Opiates
	Benzodiazepines	THC
		Phencyclidine
		Ketamine
		Nicotine

Figure 3.6 Various drugs affect the different sites along the reward pathways of the brain.

For a drug to be considered addicting, it must be capable of producing pleasure, followed by repeated drug taking so that the pleasure is re-experienced, and it must also lead to tolerance and dependence. Tolerance is defined as the need to take larger doses of a drug over time to achieve the same effect. Tolerance may be due to receptor systems in the brain becoming less sensitive to a drug over time. For example, someone who uses heroin will soon develop tolerance and will increase their dose in order to achieve the same sense of pleasure or high. The opioid receptors on cells in the midbrain that surround the VTA system may decrease in number on the post-synaptic neurons when exposed to repeated doses of heroin (receptor down-regulation). As a result there are fewer signals in the post-synaptic cells that ultimately cause the VTA system to become active. This may lead the user to take larger doses in order to occupy the remaining opioid receptors for longer periods of time. Tolerance develops very quickly with amphetamines and opiates.

Drug dependence occurs when the user must take the drug to feel normal and to avoid uncomfortable withdrawal symptoms. Specific withdrawal symptoms for each class of drugs will be discussed in the next chapter, but all drug withdrawal states include the sensation of wanting or craving the drug. During drug craving, certain areas of the reward pathways become activated in anticipation of rewards. Areas in the prefrontal cortex (dorsolateral prefrontal cortex), the amygdala, and temporal lobe become active when cocaine abusers are shown stimuli typically associated with drug use, such as a video of simulated cocaine use (Figure 3.7). This state is very powerful in addicted individuals and may lead to extreme and risky behaviors that cause significant health, social, and legal consequences.

■ **Learn more about addictive pathways in the brain** Search the Internet for *dopamine* and *motivation* or *nucleus accumbens* and *reward*.

LOSS OF BEHAVIORAL CONTROL

One of the classic signs of drug or alcohol addition is continued use despite harmful consequences. Addicted individuals will continue to use drugs or alcohol despite the mounting harmful effects to their health, family, employment, legal status, and quality of life. Earlier we discussed the brain regions and neurotransmitters involved with pleasure, drives, and reinforcement. In this chapter we will discuss the brain areas involved with decision-making and how drugs of abuse alter these areas and lead to further destructive behavior.

Drugs of abuse can cause immediate feelings of pleasure and intoxication by activating the ventral tegmental dopaminergic system. There is mounting scientific evidence that drugs also alter other brain areas that are involved with decision-making, planning, and behavioral control. Several studies have demonstrated that chronic drug use alters the brain's frontal cortex

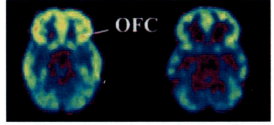

A   Normal   Cocaine addict

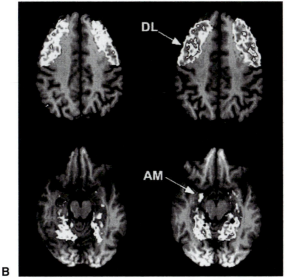

B   Noncraving state   Cocaine addict

Figure 3.7 (A) These PET scans show brain activity in a normal subject and in a cocaine addict. The cocaine addict has decreased brain activity in the orbitofrontal cortex (OFC) when compared to the normal subject. Low frontal cortex metabolism may cause the loss of behavioral control in drug addicts. **(B)** These PET scans show brain activity in a person who is craving cocaine. The scans on the right show brain activity in cocaine addicts who were exposed to cocaine paraphernalia and videos of people using cocaine. These scans show activity in the dorsolateral prefrontal cortex (DL), which is important in short-term memory, and amygdala (AM), which influences emotions and memory. In volunteers who were not exposed to non-drug-related stimuli, this brain activity was not seen (scans at left).

where we make decisions about the consequences of our actions. The frontal cortex decides on which actions to make in a particular situation by evaluating the risks and benefits of a particular action. The prefrontal region of the frontal cortex is believed to be involved in the development of addiction from early stages of use and abuse to dependence and addiction. Drugs of abuse cause the prefrontal cortex to overvalue reward, undervalue risk, and fail to learn from repeated mistakes. The mechanism of this effect is not completely understood, but there is evidence that drugs of abuse decrease the influence of the prefrontal cortex on the nucleus accumbens and other limbic areas. In other words, addiction can be due to the continuous pursuit of pleasure that is caused by the drugs affecting the midbrain dopamine systems, as well as by compulsive drug-taking and loss of behavioral control due to the drugs disrupting the frontal cortex.

Individuals addicted to methamphetamine have been studied with various behavioral tests that show that these addicted individuals made impulsive decisions based on habits and ignored the harm that their decisions can cause. Like these methamphetamine addicts, individuals with brain damage to the prefrontal cortex make choices based on the chances for immediate benefit rather than on future consequences. Therefore, the consequences of prolonged drug use include frontal cortex dysfunction that leads to choices based on short-term rewards as well as a hypersensitivity to these rewards. A drug-addicted frontal cortex is like a car speeding out of control: the driver can't hit the brakes (no behavioral control) and the driver's foot is planted on the accelerator despite impending danger (hypersensitivity to immediate gratification). It is easy to see how drug abuse is progressive when brain systems involved with behavioral control are unable to stop drug-taking behavior. (See Table 3.2 for an overview of major brain systems involved with drug abuse and addiction.)

Table 3.2 Summary of Brain Areas Implicated in Drug Addiction

BRAIN AREA	ROLE IN NORMAL BEHAVIOR	EFFECTS OF DRUGS OF ABUSE
Ventral tegmental dopamine system	Motivational system important for survival behaviors (eating drinking, reproductive behaviors)	Increase system's activity by various mechanisms
Nucleus accumbens	Subjective experience of reward and gratification; anticipation of pleasure during craving	Increase dopamine levels in NA which causes "high" and craving during drug absence
Limbic system (amygdala)	Emotional response to cues that predict reward; recalls memories of past experiences; activated during craving	Causes agitation and behavioral activation during craving; remembers pleasures of previous highs
Frontal cortex	Weighs risks and benefits of behaviors; controls actions (behavioral inhibition)	Inactivation leads to impulsive decisions and compulsive behaviors

SUMMARY POINTS

- Neurotransmitters implicated in the effects of drugs of abuse include serotonin, norepinephrine, dopamine, GABA, and specific neuropeptides.
- The ventral tegmental dopaminergic system is responsible for the pleasurable effects of drugs as well as drug craving.
- The frontal cortex is unable to control drives for drugs in addicted individuals.

4 | Stimulants and Hallucinogens

In previous chapters, we saw that each drug of abuse works a little differently in the brain. Most of the drugs reviewed in the next two chapters are considered habit forming and addicting; therefore they are known to affect the chemical motivation system in the brain (the dopamine system). The way they influence the brain and other chemical systems, besides the dopamine system, determines what effect they have on behavior. Drugs are categorized based on the way they change behavior.

For instance, stimulants (drugs that increase activity of our brain and body such as amphetamines) affect chemicals, such as norepinephrine, that keep us awake, alert, and active. Amphetamines fool the brain because their chemical structures are very similar to our neurotransmitters (Figure 4.1). On the other hand, depressants (drugs that make us sleepy and decrease body functions such as alcohol and GHB) affect brain chemical systems that normally cause feelings of tiredness or sleepiness, such as GABA. Drugs that affect our ability to sense our environment, such as **LSD** or **PCP**, alter chemical systems that may cause distortions of reality or hallucinations. Some drugs can be categorized into more than one group (such as Ecstasy, which can act like a stimulant as well as a **hallucinogen**). However, all of these drugs of abuse have the ability to change our mood and the way we think and feel.

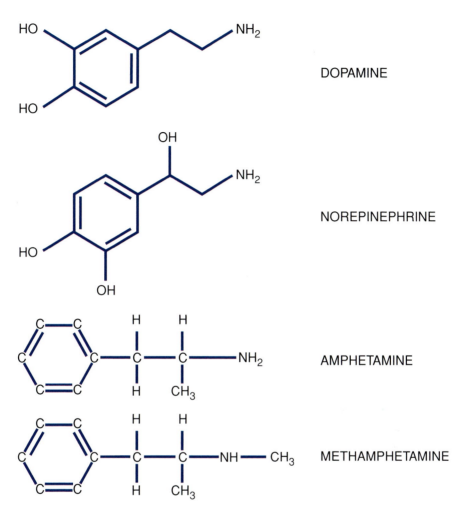

DOPAMINE

NOREPINEPHRINE

AMPHETAMINE

METHAMPHETAMINE

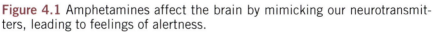

Figure 4.1 Amphetamines affect the brain by mimicking our neurotransmitters, leading to feelings of alertness.

Let's review each class of drugs and discuss the impacts they have on our brain and behavior.

STIMULANTS

Not all stimulants are alike. Although they all increase activity in the central nervous system and the body, stimulants may have

Table 4.1 Effects of Stimulant Abuse (Amphetamines and Cocaine)

SHORT-TERM EFFECTS (DURING INTOXICATION)	LONG-TERM CONSEQUENCES
Behavioral excitation (arousal, hyperactivity, excess energy, alertness, confident, talkative)	Psychosis (extreme paranoia, suspicious, aggressive)
Acute psychosis (suspicious, paranoid, hallucinations)	Weight loss
Elevation in body temperature	Poor hygiene
Increase in blood pressure	Skin lesions; hallucinations of bugs on skin
Irregular heart rhythms	Heart disease
Stroke	Risks of infections, hepatitis, anemia, and other diseases if used intravenously
Heart attack	Addiction; rebound depression (suicidal)

different addictive potentials. For instance methamphetamine or crystal meth is one of the most potent stimulants in existence. On the other hand, caffeine is one of the weakest. They both are habit forming but to very different degrees. Crystal meth is very addicting while caffeine is mildly habit forming. Why? It is because of the way they affect our brain. The quicker a drug reaches the chemical motivator system in the brain and the more it stimulates it, the more addicting it is. Let's consider the most commonly abused stimulants. (See Table 4.1 for an overview of the physical and behavioral effects of stimulant abuse.)

Amphetamines

Amphetamines are powerful stimulants and are very addicting. When abused, they over-stimulate the brain by increasing activity of the norepinephrine system (the arousal neurotransmitter). As a result of too much norepinephrine release in the hypothalamus, amphetamines cause long periods of wakefulness, decreased appetite, agitation, irritability, and increased

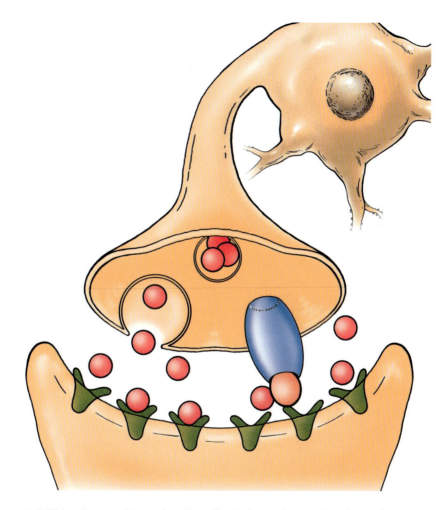

Figure 4.2 This diagram illustrates the effect of cocaine on the dopamine reuptake channel of the synapse. Cocaine blocks the reuptake of dopamine, leading to increased amounts of dopamine in the synapse.

body temperature. Amphetamines can also cause a large release of dopamine in the nucleus accumbens, the pleasure center (Figure 4.2). As a result, these drugs drive the user to take more and more of the drug to maintain the artificially high levels of dopamine.

Table 4.2 Behavioral Cycles of Stimulant Abuse

STAGE	BEHAVIORAL SIGNS
Intoxication (amphetamine or cocaine use)	Behavioral excitation (energized, aroused, etc.)
Drug elimination (negative feelings, "coming down" from high)	Restless, agitated, anxious
Repeated use (to relieve negative feelings); binge use (frequent, high doses taken)	Mania (extreme behavioral excitation); higher doses taken in attempt to achieve initial high
Crash (worsening negative feelings when drugs wear off); drug withdrawal	Depression, despair, intense drug craving, drug seeking
Return to use	Psychosis and drug toxicity become more common

Too much dopamine and norepinephrine in the frontal cortex can also cause paranoia in the user. This is called "**amphetamine psychosis**," which mimics the symptoms of paranoid schizophrenia. The paranoid user is suspicious of his or her environment and friends and may feel as though people are watching or following them. In some cases the paranoia is so severe that the user becomes violent and aggressive. Health-care workers and law enforcement officers are trained to detect the effects of amphetamines. (See Table 4.2 on the behavioral cycles of stimulant abuse.)

Amphetamines also are dangerous to the body as well as the brain. High doses of powerful stimulants can cause high blood pressure, elevated heart and breathing rates, high body temperature, strokes, and heart attacks. For these reasons methamphetamine is one of the most dangerous street drugs. It is quick acting because it is absorbed into the bloodstream and brain very quickly. It is very addicting and stimulating because it causes a large release of dopamine and norepinephrine. It is also very cheap and readily available, and its use is reaching epidemic proportions in some states. Crystal meth and other amphetamines can cause permanent damage to neurons in the frontal cortex of the brain. This type of damage to brain areas involved with behavioral inhibition makes sobriety and recovery much more difficult for these individuals. Teenage meth users with permanent brain damage are some of the most difficult cases of drug addiction (see "The Story of Skyler" box).

Cocaine

Cocaine is another powerfully addicting stimulant. Cocaine affects the same neurotransmitters as the amphetamines but uses a slightly different mechanism. While the amphetamines increase release of dopamine from the presynaptic terminals of dopamine-containing cells in the nucleus accumbens, cocaine increases the amount of dopamine in the synapse by blocking its reuptake from these presynaptic terminals (Figure 4.3). Recall from Chapter 3 that the addictive nature of certain drugs is a result of their ability to increase dopamine levels in the synapse between cells in the pleasure areas of the brain. Some drugs increase production or release of dopamine from presynaptic cells in these areas, while other drugs block the recycling of dopamine once it is released into the synapses located in these areas. Cocaine, whether snorted, injected, or smoked, is a very potent blocker of the recycling, or re-uptake, of dopamine in the nucleus accumbens. As a result, dopamine remains in the synapses of cells in the pleasure areas, causes euphoria and leads to an almost immediate drive to take more and more of the drug. Crack cocaine is a particularly addicting drug not only because of its ability to block reuptake of dopamine, but also because the drug is absorbed so rapidly from the lungs to the bloodstream and into the brain (see "Dr. Mark" box). The pharmacological and neurobiological properties of crack cocaine, in addition to its availability and affordability, have directly resulted in the social decay of many families and communities. Because cocaine and amphetamines share similar mechanisms of action in the central nervous system and body organs, **overdoses** and toxicity from cocaine and amphetamine abuse are common occurrences.

The Story of Skyler

Skyler started experimenting with drugs at age 14. Her brother introduced her to marijuana, and she soon started smoking pot occasionally with her friends. By age 16, she stared using cocaine "casually" and within another year she was using methamphetamine and crack cocaine on a daily basis. She moved to another city in an attempt to "start over" and get clean. However, she was soon back to using regularly and started injecting speed intravenously every two hours with her friends. Skyler started experiencing black-outs. One day she injected a very large dose of speed and quickly realized that she had taken too much. "I'm dead," she thought. Her eyes rolled back into her head, she convulsed, had seizures, and passed out. The next day, she was still having convulsions so she called an ambulance and spent the night in the hospital. After her discharge, she quickly went back to using. During a domestic violence call, Skyler was arrested for underage drinking and spent six days in jail where she detoxed. After her last few experiences, Skyler says that she is done with drugs. Now at age 20, she holds a job and is a full-time college student. She is healthy, responsible, and looking forward to her future. Skyler most likely inherited her compulsive behaviors (all of her brothers use drugs and her grandfather drank). She is one of a few young people who was introduced to drugs as a teenager, had a short but extensive drug use history, but so far has lived through it. When she thinks about it, she is "amazed at how ignorant people are about drugs. They'll give up their lives for it."

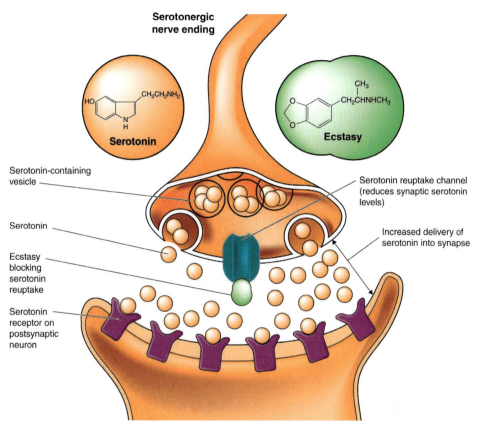

Serotonergic
nerve ending

Serotonin

Ecstasy

Serotonin-containing vesicle

Serotonin reuptake channel
(reduces synaptic serotonin levels)

Serotonin

Increased delivery of
serotonin into synapse

Ecstasy
blocking
serotonin
reuptake

Serotonin
receptor on
postsynaptic
neuron

Postsynaptic neuron

Figure 4.3 Normally, serotonin is removed from the synapse shortly after being released. Cocaine and MDMA stops this from happening, leading to increased amounts of serotonin in the synapse. This diagram shows how MDMA blocks the reuptake of serotonin.

Ecstasy (MDMA)

Ecstasy (3,4 methylenedioxymethamphetamine, MDMA) is a drug that has become increasingly popular in the last several years. As you can see from its chemical name, MDMA is a synthetic amphetamine derivative (a phenylalkylamine) and has pharmacological and behavioral properties similar to stimulants as well as hallucinogens. As a result, MDMA is often categorized

Dr. Mark

When Mark was a kid, he thought his family was normal. Later he learned that he was part of an addictive family (his mother was anorexic and his father was co-dependent). Mark had early issues with trust and self-esteem, which he compensated for by getting good grades and his parent's admiration. (He says that he also liked cough syrup—the one with alcohol in it.) After high school, Mark decided to become a doctor. He drank in college and smoked pot in med school but felt that he never had a problem. After graduating, he got his medical license, which allowed him to purchase morphine, and amphetamines through a catalog. He used the drugs occasionally. Mark then met a coke dealer and started smoking cocaine. His work suffered, but he and his partner in the medical practice covered for each other. However, within a few years it was obvious that Mark was professionally and personally unreliable and visibly sick. Soon thereafter, his family and friends held an intervention and sent him to a nationally recognized treatment center. Upon admission to the program, Mark thought that he had lost his family, his friends, and his career. But he realized he was beaten up enough and didn't want to use drugs anymore. After eight weeks, he had a spiritual moment when he finally "got it" and drugs stopped controlling his life. Mark stayed in the center for four months. When he returned home, he was pleasantly surprised to find that his friends and family were still there for him. Today, Dr. Mark runs a rehab center, is a nationally recognized addictionologist, and gives himself permission to make mistakes. "I only have to be perfect in my sobriety; I now know its OK to be human," he says. "I didn't plan on becoming a drug addict, but if I knew what would happen to my life, I wouldn't have started."

as a hallucinogen or psychedelic. MDMA not only increases norepinephrine and dopamine release like a stimulant, but it also causes a large release of serotonin. This serotonin surge is believed to cause the sense of warmth, caring, and empathy in its users. The dopamine release stimulates pleasure areas, and norepinephrine causes behavioral stimulation in MDMA users. The release of norepinephrine causes an elevation in blood pressure and heart rate and is believed to underlie the hyperactivity and energizing effect of MDMA (see Table 4.3 for a summary of the effects of MDMA). Often this drug is used in group gatherings or dances (**raves**) where the users can become dangerously hypertensive (high blood pressure), physically exhausted, and **hyperthermic** (high body temperature). Stimulants also cause stereotypical behaviors such as lip smacking, chewing, or grinding of teeth. As a result, MDMA users may place objects in their mouths to satisfy these irresistible urges.

Table 4.3 Effects of MDMA (Ecstasy)

EFFECTS	EXAMPLES
Effects on Body	Elevated body temperature, heart rate, and blood pressure; risk of heart valve damage; nausea, vomiting, and chills; muscle cramping, teeth clenching, visual disturbances; fainting; risk of loss of consciousness; possible seizures
Behavioral Effects	Initial euphoria, behavioral stimulation, empathy; rebound depression, anxiety, fatigue, irritability; chronic users experience impulsiveness, sleep and appetite problems
Brain Effects	Causes large release of serotonin followed by its depletion; chronic users may experience cognitive deficits such as difficulty with memory, attention, and mood; heavy use may lead to damage of serotonin cells and cortical gray matter
Addictive Potential	Effects on reward centers not yet completely understood; most regular MDMA users fit criteria for substance abuse diagnosis and warrant drug treatment

Tolerance and psychological dependence occur rapidly with repeated use of MDMA. MDMA has also been reported to be neurotoxic at chronic, high doses. The toxicity in the brain includes damage to the serotonin-producing cells in the dorsal raphe system. Although individuals may not suffer any immediate consequences to loss of serotonin cells, the long-term effects of this damage are unknown to researchers. It is hypothesized that the functions that are served by the serotonin system, including mood, appetite, sleep cycles, learning, and memory, may become altered as the individuals age.

■ **Learn more about how stimulants work in the brain** Search the Internet for *methamphetamine and brain mechanism, cocaine and brain mechanism,* or *MDMA and brain mechanism.*

Caffeine

Caffeine is also a psychoactive drug because it has effects on the brain and on behavior. Although caffeine can be abused and tolerance does occur, caffeine addiction, as defined by the loss of control of self-administration and the resulting negative social, legal, or health consequences, is rare. The mechanism of action of caffeine in the brain is different from that of all other stimulants. Caffeine inhibits the action of **adenosine**, a neurotransmitter that normally decreases the activity of norepinephrine cells. As a result, caffeine increases brain activity and alertness by elevating norepinephrine release in the brain. Caffeine also increases blood pressure, heart rate, respiration rate, and metabolic rate, as well as causing blood vessel constriction. If people who are tolerant to caffeine and usually need large doses in order to stay awake stop taking the drug, they may experience rebound blood vessel dilation and painful headaches as well as fatigue. (See "Caffeine: The New Drug of Abuse?" box.)

Nicotine

Nicotine is also a psychoactive stimulant and is one of the most powerfully addicting drugs in the world. (See Table 4.4 for an overview of the criteria that classify nicotine as an addictive chemical.) It is found in preparations of the tobacco leaf and is often consumed through cigarette smoke and chewing tobacco. Smoking, or inhalation, is the quickest way drugs can enter the central nervous system. The cigarette is a very effective drug delivery device. Once inhaled, nicotine in tobacco smoke can

Caffeine: The New Drug of Abuse?

The consumption of caffeinated beverages in the last few years has increased dramatically. Specialty coffee shops and espresso stands have appeared everywhere. In our homes, we order coffee beans from all over the world, store them in special containers, and grind them in expensive machines. The average cup of coffee contains 100 mg of caffeine, and the average soda has 50 mg. It is not uncommon for individuals to consume more than 500 mg of caffeine per day or more. Caffeine is now found in sport and energy drinks (along with other stimulating herbal additives) in very high concentrations. It is even in certain alcoholic beverages. The long-term effects of high caffeine intake are not known, but caffeine increases cellular metabolism, heart rate, blood pressure, and insulin secretion, and has been implicated in cardiovascular and intestinal diseases. Teenagers and children may take hidden doses of caffeine in candy and sweets (in the form of chocolate). Tolerance and dependence occur with caffeine consumption but whether it causes true addiction is debatable. The next few years should shed some light on this question as marketing campaigns, caffeine extraction devices, and caffeine preparations become more effective.

Table 4.4 Cigarette Smoking as Addictive Behavior

CRITERIA FOR NICOTINE AS ADDICTIVE SUBSTANCE	EXAMPLES
Dependence	Psychological (craving of cigarettes in particular setting) and physical dependence (withdrawal symptoms occur when use stops) develop rapidly with continual use
Tolerance	Increases in doses to achieve same effect (from one cigarette to one or two packs a day is common sequence of events)
Addiction	Use despite harm (use continues despite educational campaigns, documented effects on multiple organ systems, and medical and governmental warnings); denial
Withdrawal	Abrupt cessation of use precipitates withdrawal symptoms (agitation, irritability, craving, drug-seeking behaviors)

reach the brain's pleasure areas in less than 10 seconds. Nicotine has been reported to increase the release of dopamine in these areas as well as inhibit the activity of **monoamine oxidase** (MAO). MAO is an enzyme that metabolizes dopamine. By decreasing MAO activity, nicotine can elevate dopamine levels. As a result, the user can experience the dopamine-induced euphoria of nicotine and continual need to self-administer the drug. Nicotine is different from most stimulants because it also acts on **acetylcholine** receptors in the central and peripheral nervous systems. An increase in cholinergic activity in the brain is partly responsible for the activating, or stimulating, property of the drug. Nicotine use and dependence can lead to a serious addiction and significant health consequences. Approximately 500,000 Americans die each year from smoking, and more than 3,000 children and teenagers start smoking each day.

THE HALLUCINOGENS

This broad class of drugs includes several different compounds that alter brain function using different mechanisms of action. They all, however, have the ability to induce illusions (a mistaken perception), delusions (a mistaken idea), hallucinations (sensing something that does not exist), or to cause severe breaks with reality. Drugs in this category can affect several different neurotransmitters including serotonin. From Chapter 3, recall that serotonin controls our mood, appetite, sleep cycles, and memory, as well as sensation. Inhibiting the serotonin systems in certain areas of the brain can cause visual, auditory, or somatosensory distortions.

LSD

Lysergic acid diethylamide (LSD) is a synthetic (man-made) chemical and is one of the most potent psychoactive drugs. It is biologically active in the microgram range (one millionth of a gram). In addition to hallucinations or illusions, the user may also experience extreme anxiety, breaks with reality, and confusion. LSD also increases heart rate, blood pressure, and respiratory rate, and it causes dilation of the pupils because of its effects on the release of norepinephrine in the brain and body. Interestingly, LSD and most other hallucinogens do not significantly increase dopamine release in the pleasure areas of the brain. As a result, the addictive behaviors typically associated with most drugs of abuse do not occur with some hallucinogens. Most users take these drugs for their effects on perception and sensation and not for their reinforcing or rewarding properties.

Psilocybin and Mescaline

Two naturally occurring hallucinogens are **psilocybin**, found in certain species of mushrooms, and **mescaline**, found in peyote and other cacti. Psilocybin is similar in structure and activity to

LSD. It causes distortions of reality and perception by disturbing the serotonin system and it also causes stimulation of the brain resulting from norepinephrine release. Psilocybin is not as potent as LSD and causes less anxiety and fewer panic reactions, but it may also cause the user to feel nauseated. However, nausea and vomiting is more common with the use of mescaline. Mescaline is most commonly found in the peyote cactus and has been used as a hallucinogen for many centuries by Native American cultures in religious ceremonies. Mescaline is chemically related to amphetamine and norepinephrine and, as a result, causes stimulation and activation of the central nervous system. Mescaline causes profound nausea and vomiting and is also believed to cause disruption of the serotonin systems, which leads to more visual hallucinations than LSD or psilocybin. Synthetic mescaline has also been found to be distributed in the form of pills or capsules and is typically much more potent than the naturally occurring form.

PCP and Ketamine

Phencyclidine (PCP) and its derivative, ketamine, are very unique hallucinogenic drugs of abuse. PCP was originally marketed as an anesthetic and has been replaced with ketamine for use in veterinarian practices. These drugs affect a large number of neurotransmitters including **glutamate** (an excitatory neurotransmitter) and norepinephrine and cause **analgesia**, amnesia, **anesthesia**, confusion, excitement, agitation, hallucinations and, in high doses, a psychotic state resembling schizophrenia. These drugs are also called **dissociative** anesthetics in that they can cause the user to feel separated from his or her body and environment. These drugs are also believed to stimulate reward areas in the brain, which leads to repeated self-administration. Ketamine (also known as "special K") has become popular as a "club drug" in the rave subculture. Most supplies of these drugs are diverted from veterinarian and medical settings and are often mixed with other hallucinogenic or **cannabinoid** substances.

■ **Learn more about hallucinogens** Search the Internet for *club drug addiction* or *hallucinogens and brain.*

SUMMARY POINTS

- Stimulants increase behavioral arousal and activity by increasing the levels of norepinephrine in brain synapses.
- MDMA (Ecstasy) increases release of serotonin into synapses and has significant physical effects on the body.
- Nicotine is a powerfully addictive chemical that increases synaptic dopamine by several different mechanisms.
- Most hallucinogens act on serotonin systems in the brain. Ketamine affects several different neurotransmitters including glutamate.

5 | Depressants and Marijuana

All drugs that cause a general slowing of the central nervous system are most often categorized as depressants. All depressants cause sedation by increasing the activity of inhibitory neurotransmitters, such as gamma aminobutyric acid (GABA). GABA is found throughout the central nervous system, which is why all depressants cause a general slowing of all brain functions.

ALCOHOL

Alcohol increases the activity of GABA, as well as the endogenous opioid systems in the brain, which cause euphoria and a general sense of well-being. Recall that opioid cells surround dopamine-producing cells in the brain's motivation systems. By increasing GABA signals throughout the brain, alcohol also interferes with muscle coordination (motor cortex and **cerebellum**), speech (left hemisphere language areas), vision (occipital cortex), and planning (frontal cortex), among other functions. (See Table 5.1 for a description of alcohol intoxication as well as the common withdrawal symptoms.) Alcohol also causes relief from anxiety and often releases inhibitions in users. This, in addition to its legal distribution and socially acceptable consumption, is one reason that alcoholism and

Table 5.1 Signs of Alcohol Intoxication and Withdrawal Symptoms

INTOXICATION SIGNS	WITHDRAWAL SYMPTOMS
Initial behavioral stimulation	Behavioral agitation; irritability
Relaxation	Nervousness
Increased reaction time; driving impaired	Nausea; vomiting*
Poor motor control; unsteady; imbalanced	Increased heart rate;* shortness of breath*
Slurred speech; sedation*	Fever;* chills
Coma;* death	Hallucinations; seizures*

* Denotes life-threatening sign or symptom that requires medical treatment

Table 5.2 Early Warning Signs of Drinking Problems

Drinking several times per week
More alcohol consumed per event
Gulping drinks; binge drinking
Traffic violation; DUIs
Attempts to cut down drinking fail
Spouse or family complains
Hiding drinking; guilt and shame
Denial when confronted
Continued use despite medical, legal, and social consequences

alcohol-related disorders are so prevalent. (See Table 5.2 for a list of common warning signs of a drinking problem.)

Physical consequences of alcohol abuse include liver disease, heart and vascular changes, and esophageal, stomach, and intestinal disease. In addition, chronic alcohol abuse can lead to permanent brain damage. Certain areas of the brain, such as the thalamus, are very sensitive to the toxic effects of alcohol and are affected by the malnutrition that often occurs in alcoholics. As a result, alcoholics may suffer from **Korsakoff's syndrome** (a neurological disorder that is characterized by memory defects), cerebral and cerebellar degeneration (which leads to problems with higher **cognitive** functions and motor control, respectively) as well as suffer from physical health problems (see "Buster and His New Liver" box).

Buster and His New Liver

Buster always associated drinking with having a good time. When he was a kid, his parents would drink with friends and give him a sip every so often. When he was 11, his mother died. Buster remembered that alcohol was for happiness and soon started drinking to combat his feelings of loneliness and fear. As a teenager, he drank and had drinking contests with his friends to be cool. By age 13 he was having black-outs, and by 17 he was using pot and other drugs. Buster even used some intravenous drugs but his main drug was alcohol. In his early 20s Buster married an alcoholic, and was smoking cocaine by his early 30s. After a divorce, he remarried and went back to school. His non-stop drinking continued until his second wife moved out. One day after she left, he had a moment of clarity and realized that if he continued his lifestyle he might not survive. He went to his first Alcoholics Anonymous (AA) meeting that day and has been going ever since. However, while Buster was in recovery his health began to decline. He was diagnosed with hepatitis C and cirrhosis, and in 2005 he received a liver transplant. "I'm not sure if my liver failed from drinking or I.V. drugs or vaccines I got in Vietnam," says Buster. "I do know that I learned in recovery that it was OK to have problems and that I have found new hope in my life." Buster is thankful every day for his sobriety and grateful for his new lease on life.

Table **5.3** Effects of Prescription Depressants, GHB, and Rohypnol®

INTOXICATION AND SHORT-TERM EFFECTS	COMPLICATIONS OF CONTINUED USE
Impaired decision-making and intellectual functions	Abuse can quickly lead to dependency
Reduced short-term memory; blackouts	Insomnia (can't sleep without drug)
Lack of coordination and balance	Use leads to rapid tolerance; acquiring from non-medical or illegal sources
Sleepiness; slurred speech	Life-threatening withdrawal symptoms (seizures)
Rapid sedation and overdose	Increases risks of falls or motor vehicle accidents
Death from respiratory failure	Elderly are particularly susceptible to all types of depressants

PRESCRIPTION DEPRESSANTS

Not all addictive drugs are illegal. Some prescription drugs can cause dependency and addiction if overused or used against the advice of the prescribing clinician. One class of prescription depressants includes the **sedative-hypnotics**. This class includes drugs such as Valium®, Librium®, Xanax®, and other benzodiazepines (Valium®-like drugs) and is typically used for anxiety disorders as well as insomnia. These medications are powerful GABA agonists (increase GABA activity) and they also affect the dopaminergic motivational systems in the brain, which can lead to self-administration and dependence. In addition, these medications cause general sedative effects that include disruption of brain circuits involved with balance and motor control, sensation and perception, and planning and judgment (Table 5.3). In high doses, sedative-hypnotics can cause overwhelming GABA activation which leads to loss of consciousness and amnesia. When mixed with alcohol or other sedatives, this class of drugs can often lead to respiratory depression, coma, and death.

GHB

Gamma hydroxybutyrate (GHB) was originally sold as a nutritional supplement and marketed as a muscle growth enhancer, a result of its weak stimulation of growth-hormone release. It quickly became popular as a depressant and a drug of abuse. However, GHB is a quick-acting, powerful sedative. It is colorless, odorless, tasteless, and very potent when mixed with alcohol. People under the influence of GHB lose behavioral inhibitions very quickly, become easily manipulated, and often forget what they did while intoxicated. As a result, it has become popular as a "**date-rape**" **drug**. GHB is very similar in structure to GABA and therefore increases inhibitory signals in the brain. Users become lethargic, fatigued, and sleepy. They often slur their speech and their balance becomes unsteady. Overdoses causing coma and death from respiratory failure are common because of the quick and powerful effects of the drug. GHB stimulates the dopaminergic reward pathways and pleasure areas and is therefore considered an addictive drug. Physical dependence, tolerance, and addiction to GHB are common with chronic use.

ROHYPNOL

Rohypnol® (flunitrazepam; also known as "roofies") is also a short-acting, powerful sedative and depressant in the benzodiazepine family of drugs (Figure 5.1). It is similar to GHB in its pharmacological and behavioral effects. It is very powerful when mixed with alcohol and has also been used as a date-rape drug. Physical dependence, tolerance, addiction, its mechanism of action, and the potential for overdose are very similar to that of GHB. There are no **antidotes** for overdose from GHB or

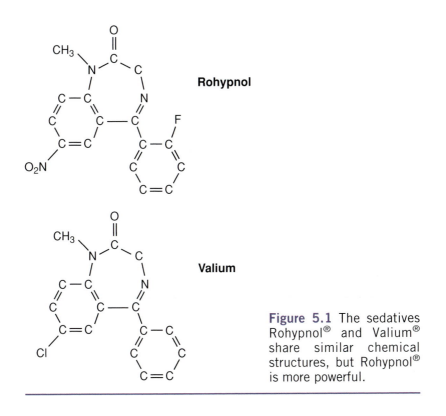

Figure 5.1 The sedatives Rohypnol® and Valium® share similar chemical structures, but Rohypnol® is more powerful.

Rohypnol. There is no safe medication that can be given to reverse the respiratory depression or coma that can occur with acute toxicity of these powerful GABA agonists. The only medical treatment is respiratory support via a ventilator and to wait for the drug to be metabolized.

INHALANTS

Inhalants are solvents or aerosols that are inhaled and absorbed through the lungs into the bloodstream. Because of their route of administration, inhalants have an almost immediate effect on the brain and body. These chemicals are found in common products such as spray paint, glue, cement, gasoline, nail polish remover, and pressurized chemicals (Table 5.4). Because of their easy availability, this class of drugs is often abused by younger teenagers and

Table 5.4 Commonly Used Inhalants and Their Ingredients

INHALANT	INGREDIENTS
Aerosols	Freon, toluene, xylene
Degreasing agents; spray paint and paint thinners; rubber cement	Benzene, butyl acetate, heptane, hexane, methylene chloride, naphthalene, toluene, xylene
Typewriter correction fluid	Trichloroethylene
Laughing gas	Nitrous oxide
Room deodorizers	Amyl nitrite, isobutyl nitrite
Gasoline	Gasoline and octane fuel additives
Lighter fluid	Butane, isopropane

children. These products contain toluene, propane, butane, acetone, nitrous oxide, or various fluorocarbons. Because these chemicals are vaporous and very soluble in fat, they are absorbed very quickly by all biological tissues once inhaled.

Users may experience a brief period of excitation (behavioral activity) followed by sedation (drowsiness) and **disinhibition** in the user. The individual may then experience drowsiness, dizziness, imbalance, slurred speech, and will appear drunk. The mechanism of action of this class of drugs is not completely known but they mimic the effects of anesthetics and alcohol in the brain. Inhalants may disrupt the membranes that surround all neurons and thereby cause general sedation and anesthesia. In addition, these chemicals may directly increase the action of GABAergic cells in the brain, which may lead to additional sedation and drowsiness. Inhalants also increase activation of the motivational dopaminergic system, which causes euphoria and may lead to chronic self-dosing and addiction.

Not only do these chemicals disrupt normal activity of brain cells, but inhalants can quickly disrupt other biologically excitable cells located in other organs such as the heart. There have been numerous reports of sudden and fatal heart attacks resulting from **sudden cardiac arrhythmias** in children following the inhalation of volatile solvents and aerosols. Chronic abuse of inhalants has been shown to cause permanent cell loss in the central and peripheral nervous systems, which may lead to muscle weakness, numbness, and instability.

■ **Learn more about the depressants** Search the Internet for *CNS depressants and brain, alcohol abuse, date rape drugs,* or *inhalant abuse.*

OPIATES

The opiates are a separate class of drugs that have very specific mechanisms of action. All opiates bind to their own separate set of receptors in the brain (endorphin and enkephalin receptors). This is unusual for most types of drugs of abuse. Most of the **psychoactive** drugs have their effects on the brain and our behavior by altering other neurotransmitter systems (the stimulants increase norepinephrine; depressants use GABA; hallucinogens alter serotonin, etc.). Opiates, however, bind specific opioid receptors in certain areas of the central nervous system as well as other organ systems.

PRESCRIPTION PAINKILLERS

The most common use for prescription opiates is for analgesia, to decrease the sensation of pain. These medications block pain signals from damaged tissue in the body when opioid receptors in the brain are occupied by these opiates. These drugs are effective as painkillers. However, opioid receptors are also located on cells that control the chemical motivational system that uses dopamine. When drugs like heroin, morphine, codeine, opium, and prescription painkillers such as OxyContin® and Vicodin®, turn on these opioid receptors, the user may feel euphoria and pleasure as well as relief from pain. Because of this effect on the pleasure pathways, these drugs can be addicting. Indeed, some of the most addicting substances, such as heroin and **fentanyl**, belong to this class of drugs. (See "William's Story" box.)

HEROIN

Heroin is a very addicting opiate. Chemically, it consists of two molecules of morphine joined together which make it more soluble in fat (**lipophilic**) and is therefore absorbed into the

William's Story

William was studious as a kid. Quiet and reserved, he preferred music and sports to partying with friends. In high school, he started smoking pot mostly just to fit in with his peers. In college, William had his first experience with painkillers after an eye injury. Immediately he thought, "now I know what it's like to be on heroin." He felt extremely euphoric, confident, and calm. Over a five-year period, he had a couple of minor surgeries and injuries that exposed him to painkillers again. After his wisdom teeth were pulled the following year, he said he was soon "taking them at all costs. I lost everything—girlfriends, the trust of my parents, my health, and thousands of dollars. I spent days driving around to different doctors, faking injuries, even asking my friends for their drugs." If he couldn't get opiates, he would drink to keep the withdrawal symptoms away. Finally, William got help. With the support of his friends, parents, and employer, William went through intensive in-patient treatment and is now healthy and productive. He recommends, "breaking out of your thinking that you want and need things all of the time; improve yourself. It doesn't matter if you're rich or poor, Ivy League grad, or high school dropout; because if you think you have a problem—you do."

bloodstream and brain easily. Heroin is most often intra-venously injected, but it may also be sniffed or snorted into the nose. Because of the recent trend in snorting heroin, more young people who were dissuaded by the stigma associated with needle use are now trying heroin. Regardless of the route of administration, users can progress from experimentation to abuse and addiction very quickly. Heroin reaches the pleasure pathways in the brain rapidly and causes a significant increase in the production and release of dopamine into the nucleus accumbens. (See "The Case of the Frozen Addicts" box.)

The physical effects of opiates are caused when the drugs bind to opioid receptors in bodily tissues as well as in the brain. When people are under the influence of an opiate, their pupils become very constricted, they may experience itching of their skin because of histamine release, become constipated and feel nauseated, and their blood pressure, pulse, and breathing may decrease. Overdose from opiates causes respiratory depression, which occurs when the breathing centers of the brain become insensitive to carbon dioxide, a normal stimulus to inhale air. Because overdose is directly due to opioid receptor binding, the use of opiate receptor blockers (such as **naloxone**) is an effective emergency treatment for opiate overdose. Tolerance and dependence also occur rapidly with continual use of opiates. As a result, individuals can become addicted to prescription opiates as well as illegal opiates very quickly. (Table 5.5)

THE CANNABINOIDS: MARIJUANA

The cannabinoids are derived from cannabis plants (marijuana). Much has been written about the social, legal, medical, and historical implications of marijuana. However, the neurobiology of marijuana and one of its active ingredients, delta-9-tetrahydocannabinol, or THC, has been studied extensively. Marijuana preparations are typically smoked or sometimes ingested in food. THC is very fat soluble and therefore enters the bloodstream and brain very quickly. Recent scientific evidence suggests that THC does increase dopamine release in the nucleus accumbens. These data imply that repeated use of

The Case of the Frozen Addicts

In the mid-1980s, several medical reports surfaced about heroin users who were found in immobile but conscious states in their homes after using heroin. One by one they were brought into emergency rooms by friends or family members. For days the doctors were puzzled as to why these individuals suddenly could not move or speak. One patient had a slight tremor of one of his extremities so, as a last resort, the doctors tried a Parkinson's medication to relieve his condition. As the medication took effect, the patient began to move and speak and explain what had happened to him. He and all the other "frozen" addicts had bought what they thought was synthetic heroin from drug dealers. The dealers had bought the drug from a chemist who made mistakes in the synthesis of the heroin and instead of making meperidine (an opiate), he made a previously unknown neurotoxin called MPTP. When the heroin users took the drug, the toxin caused massive damage to the substantia nigra, a dopamine system in the brain used for muscle movement. (This system is the same chemical system that is destroyed over many decades in patients with Parkinson's disease.) However, in these drug users, the substantia nigra was almost completely destroyed in a few days from a single accidental exposure to MPTP. While these individuals still suffer from profound Parkinsonism, what was learned from these events is twofold: MPTP is a useful research tool for the scientific development of Parkinson's medications, and the synthesis of designer drugs (such as synthetic meperidine, methamphetamine, and MDMA) is unregulated and extremely dangerous.

Table 5.5 Signs and Symptoms of Opiate Use and Withdrawal (Includes Heroin, Morphine, and Prescription Painkillers)

PHYSICAL AND PSYCHOLOGICAL EFFECTS OF OPIATES	WITHDRAWAL SYMPTOMS (OPPOSITE OF INTOXICATION EFFECTS)*
Sleepiness	Insomnia
Sedation; motor inhibition	Agitation; muscle cramps and exaggerated reflexes
Euphoria (pleasure)	Depression; anxiety
Pinpoint pupils	Dilated pupils
Slow heart rate; low blood pressure	Rapid pulse; high blood pressure
Decreased stomach and intestinal activity (constipation)	Diarrhea; vomiting
Analgesia (pain relief)	Bone, joint, and muscle pain
Decreased glandular secretions	Yawning, tearing, and runny nose
Respiratory depression (overdose can cause death)	Panting; increased breathing rate

* Withdrawal symptoms are uncomfortable but not typically life threatening

marijuana can be addicting. This increased level of dopamine release associated with THC is relatively minor, however, when compared with the increase in dopamine levels caused by more addicting drugs such as cocaine, crystal meth, and heroin. Nonetheless, smoking marijuana can become habit forming and classified as addictive. There have been reports of physical dependence on THC to the point that individuals have suffered physical withdrawal symptoms when they stop using marijuana. These withdrawal symptoms are very similar to opiate withdrawal symptoms and include irritability, depression, tearing, diarrhea, rapid heart rate, and elevated blood pressure. Because of this similarity in withdrawal symptoms, cannabinoid preparations are sometimes categorized as opiates and not in a separate class or as hallucinogens or depressants.

Table 5.6 Mechanisms of Health Risks of Marijuana Abuse

RISK OR CONSEQUENCE	MECHANISM
Bronchitis, lung irritation, lung damage	Marijuana smoke; carcinogens
Mild analgesia; appetite stimulation	Binding of THC to opiate-like anandamide receptors in midbrain and hypothalamus
Fatigue, apathy, impaired concentration (amotivational syndrome)	THC's effects on midbrain, limbic, and cortical regions of the brain
Impaired short-term memory	THC's effects on limbic system (including hippocampus)
Psychological and physical dependence	THC activating the ventral tegmental dopaminergic system
Opiate-like withdrawal symptoms during abstinence	Unoccupied anandamide receptors precipitate withdrawal syndrome

In addition to sharing properties with opiates, THC also has been shown to possess its own binding sites and receptors in the brain. This indicates that the brain must have its own, naturally occurring neurotransmitter that can normally occupy these receptors. Scientists have isolated that chemical (**anandamide**) and found its receptors in the pleasure areas as well as in the hippocampus, an area of the brain important for memory formation. Physical effects from marijuana preparations include bloodshot eyes, drooping eyelids, elevated heart rate, and high blood pressure. Psychological effects include hunger, relaxation, occasional anxiety or paranoia, **internalization** and feelings of detachment, and impaired coordination and perception. These latter effects can disrupt reaction times and interfere with normal decision making. Long-term effects of marijuana smoking include lung damage and possible damage to cell layers in the hippocampus (Table 5.6).

Marijuana preparations have been used for medicinal purposes in the treatment of glaucoma, nausea, and poor appetite. THC decreases ocular pressure (pressure in the eyeball) and therefore benefited some glaucoma patients. THC also stimulates anandamide receptors in the brain stem and therefore may help chemotherapy patients suffering from nausea and vomiting. THC also stimulates hypothalamic centers and increases appetite and hunger in chemotherapy patients as well as in patients suffering from AIDS-wasting syndrome.

■ **Learn more about the opiates and marijuana** Search the Internet for *heroin use*, *painkiller abuse*, or *marijuana abuse*.

SUMMARY POINTS

- All depressants cause central nervous system sedation by increasing the actions of the inhibitory neurotransmitter GABA.
- Opiates act through a specific set of opioid receptors in the brain normally activated by neuropeptides.
- One of the psychoactive ingredients in marijuana is THC, which binds to specific receptors in the limbic system and pathways involved with appetite and the sensation of pain.

6 | The Cycle of Addiction

Individuals start using drugs for various reasons including curiosity, peer pressure, and drug availability. It is very difficult to predict who will become an addict; certainly nobody *wants* to become an addict. The most recent scientific evidence supports the notion that addiction is a biogenetic, psychosocial brain disease. In other words, whether or not an individual progresses from casual use to abuse and drug addiction depends on several biological and social variables. Do addiction or other compulsive behaviors run in an individual's family? In what kind of an environment was an individual raised? Was it loving and nurturing or stressful and isolated? Could the individual's possible future addictive tendencies be identified earlier in life? In this chapter, we will examine how these variables influence brain areas underlying addictive behavior and the progression from initial curiosity to compulsive addiction.

NATURE (HEREDITY AND GENETICS)

Our genes not only determine our height, eye, and hair color, but also our tendency to engage in compulsive behaviors. The influence of genetics on addictive behaviors has been studied in genetically identical twins raised in the same family, twins that have been raised by different families, and even in genetically selected animal models. Overall, the studies suggest that genetics contribute to approximately 50 to 60% of all cases of addiction. These studies have also investigated family histories and have shown that if one of your parents is an alcoholic, your chances of becoming an alcoholic increase by one-third. If both parents are alcoholic, your chances quadruple. If both parents and a grandparent are alcoholic, your chances are nine times more likely.

Genetic studies have also identified specific genes associated with alcoholism. Not surprisingly, these genes encode for proteins in cells located in the ventral tegmental dopaminergic system, particularly dopamine receptors. It is hypothesized that individuals with these genes have exaggerated positive responses to their initial exposures to drugs or alcohol. This initial positive response has been associated with drug dependence later in life (see "Mary's Honesty" box). These studies have suggested the same exaggerated response to other potentially compulsive activities such as gambling, sexual behavior, and overeating. However, it is important to remember that one need not have a genetic predisposition to addiction to progress to some type of addiction. Many individuals whose parents did not drink still become alcoholics. Therefore, other factors must play a role in the development of drug or alcohol addiction.

NURTURE (THE ROLE OF THE ENVIRONMENT)

The context or environment in which we are raised can have tremendous impact on our future behavior as well as our brain development. Individuals who are raised in environments that provide emotional support, love, adequate nutrition, and where learning and healthy lifestyles are encouraged have reduced rates of drug and alcohol abuse. A common saying is that the brain is like a muscle—use it or lose it. The more we engage different areas of our brains in positive, healthy behaviors, such as learning new information, patience, and delayed gratification, the greater the likelihood these brain areas will remain vital into

Mary's Honesty

Mary's dad was an alcoholic, and her mom was a social drinker. There was a lot of drinking in her house while she was growing up but she didn't try alcohol until she was 12. One night when Mary was alone at home for the first time, she raided the liquor cabinet, and later that night ended up vomiting in a snow bank. Despite her first negative experience while under the influence of alcohol, Mary continued to drink. She started drinking small amounts from each liquor bottle and by age 14, she was having black-outs. Mary's mom stayed off her back because she was mainly worried about Mary's dad, who was drinking heavily by this time. By her senior year in high school, Mary was drinking morning, noon, and night. She knew her problem was worsening but thought it was because of the stress of her home life. Mary continued her heavy drinking throughout her college years (she now admits that her drinking certainly limited her intellectual abilities and opportunities). While Mary was in college, her dad got sober and told her to stop, too. She slowed down and "only" binged as a reward for hard school work. In grad school, she got the "drunkest student" award, and while on a trip overseas, Mary experienced her "low point" one night after throwing up in a bush. So she slowed down again and "only" smoked pot for a while. Soon she was drinking again and now claims she had no "off-switch. If I had one drink, I would end up drunk. Every day I started counting down to my next drink." One New Year's Day she realized she had to stop. Mary finally made it through all the years of denial and has been sober for 12 years. "Don't wait too long to stop," warns Mary. "And never forget to be honest with yourself."

adulthood. For some individuals who are raised in emotionally painful, stressful environments, however, drugs, alcohol, or some other addicting behaviors or substances may provide an escape from the emotional pain and stress that they endure daily. Individuals who are raised in such stressful situations have much higher rates of addictive behaviors.

■ **Learn more about the cause of addictive behaviors** Search the Internet for *genetics of alcoholism* or *addiction and stress*.

The mechanism by which stress and addiction interact is beginning to be understood. It is believed that environmental stress **primes** the brain for addictive behaviors. Stress can alter dopamine cells in the VTA to become more responsive to exposure to a drug that affects the system. This may help to explain why environmental stress causes an individual to progress from casual drug use to abuse and addiction more quickly than someone raised in a less stressful environment.

The rate at which an individual progresses from initial drug exposure to casual use to abuse and addiction depends not only on their genetics and environment but also on their psychoactive drug use. If an individual has a genetic predisposition and experiences emotional stress, then they will probably progress rapidly once psychoactive drug use starts. All three factors interact with one another. For instance, if an individual has a lower level of genetic susceptibility, then additional stress or use of stronger psychoactive drugs would be required for that individual to progress at a rapid rate. The rate of progression can vary from person to person. It may take one person several years of alcohol abuse before they become truly addicted; it may take another person less than a year if alcoholism runs in their family. On the other hand, an individual raised in an abusive environment may quickly progress from cocaine use once a month, for example, to several times a day in a few weeks.

EARLY BEHAVIOR PREDICTS FUTURE PROBLEMS

Recent scientific studies suggest that problems with behavioral self-control arising in early childhood are signs that the individual may be susceptible to drug abuse later in life. This suggests that areas in the frontal cortex responsible for self-control, decision-making, and goal-directed behavior exhibit signs of dysfunction early in life. These signs include irritability and the expression of intense emotions; these individuals have a harder time returning to a quiet emotional state after an outburst. Other childhood symptoms include lack of behavioral control such as acting out, being disruptive, defying authority, and impulsiveness. Studies are being done to investigate a possibility that a lack of frontal cortical control is responsible for these behaviors. Future studies may identify ways to practice improvements in frontal lobe function so as to promote behavioral inhibition, self-control, and possibly protect against future vulnerability to drug abuse.

Mental disorders may also exist with drug and alcohol abuse later in life. As many as 60% of individuals who abuse drugs and alcohol also suffer from a mental illness such as depression, manic depression, and schizophrenia. Since substance use and mental disorders can co-exist, it is often difficult to determine which comes first. Individuals who suffer from the symptoms of depression or schizophrenia may start to use drugs to relieve some of their uncomfortable symptoms. This may then lead them to drug addiction and further problems with their mental illness. Other studies have indicated that substance abuse may start first and then unmask, or lead to, mental illnesses (Table 6.1).

BRAIN AND BEHAVIOR IN THE PROGRESSION FROM ADDICTION TO RECOVERY

There are several identifiable behaviors that typically occur in the progression towards drug addiction. It is important to

Table 6.1 Where to Get Help

WHO OR WHERE	WHAT TO EXPECT
Your primary care clinician (family doctor)	Screening questionnaires Diagnosis Referrals to specialists Overall medical management of recovery
Specialty clinicians (addictionists)	Certified to treat addictions; knowledgeable of local resources and steps in recovery; can treat withdrawal symptoms
Hospital or crisis center	Assess extent of problem Recommend treatment plan
Local yellow pages or behavioral health directory • under "Drug Abuse and Addiction Information and Treatment" • or "Alcoholism Information and Treatment"	Location of community resources (crisis centers, detox, or rehab facilities, counselors, group meetings, etc.)
Internet • Alcoholics Anonymous • National Institute on Drug Abuse	Useful information about substance abuse and treatment; review of neural mechanisms and drug information
Individual therapist	Identification of risk factor Cognitive behavioral therapy
Group therapy	Sharing experiences and hope with similar individuals

understand the changes that occur in the brain during this progression so that these changes can be treated and reversed during the recovery stage. Addiction and recovery stages were first developed by E. M. Jellinek in the early 1940s in order to categorize different types of alcoholics and to underscore the notion that drug and alcohol addiction are the results of a brain disorder and are not due to weaknesses of will or moral character. The medical community has since accepted the concept that addiction is a brain disease.

In the progression from initial drug use to abuse to addiction and recovery, there are several key steps that occur in the brain that coincide with behavioral changes. Let's follow a hypothetical individual (Bill) through various stages of substance abuse and recovery and outline some of the brain changes that may underlie his behavior.

Bill didn't start using drugs or alcohol until he was in his 20s; early experimentation didn't lead to immediate compulsive behavior. None of his family members were alcohol or drug users; he didn't have a strong genetic predisposition, but Bill liked the effects. Bill drank more often as he got older and started drinking more at parties. Alcohol made him feel relaxed and at ease as a result of ethanol's action at GABA receptors in the cortex and limbic system. It also made him happy as ethanol caused dopamine release in the nucleus accumbens; neuropeptide release reinforces this effect. Occasionally alcohol made him more social, confident, and talkative from the ethanol's sedation of the cerebral cortex, which resulted in a release of emotions from limbic system—cortical disinhibition. Bill found that if he had a particularly bad day or was stressed at work that he would have a couple of drinks on his way home. His environmental stress increased use; repeated stress signals prime reward pathways. He noticed that he started to look forward to the pleasure that alcohol would give him and was a little edgy until he had his first drink. The prediction of reward increased dopamine release which caused behavioral stimulation to locate and acquire the reward.

At this point, Bill's behavior was becoming more patterned and he was transitioning from recreational use to habituation. When he stopped at the bar after work, he noticed that he was increasing the amount that he was drinking and that he started to like the effects more and more. He needed to have more alcohol to improve his mood and feel relaxed. Bill was developing tolerance; neurotransmitter adaptation was occurring in the brain; and his liver enzymes were also becoming more effective in metabolizing ethanol. Over the last couple of months he gained weight and ate less nutritional meals. Alcohol is high in calories, which caused his weight gain and meal skipping. Bill felt worse throughout the day, which caused him to drink more in the evenings. Habitual alcohol use alters serotonin systems, which leads to mood instability. Bill also noticed that he was getting more headaches and feeling unusually tired the mornings after he drank. (Alcohol disrupts normal sleep cycles.)

On several occasions, Bill's family and friends reminded him of things he did while he was drinking. Bill laughed along with the stories but only remembered some things that he did. Bill was experiencing black-outs: short-term memory systems in the limbic system are sedated by alcohol's GABAergic and anesthetic properties. These experiences caused Bill to feel guilty about his behavior and, for a short period of time, he cut down on his drinking. However, continued stress at work and at home caused Bill to start returning to the bar after work. Within weeks he was drinking more than when he stopped before. He was experiencing more black-outs and his efforts to control his drinking failed. Bill lost interest in things that he used to enjoy, even his hobbies. He tried to avoid his family and friends and tended to isolate himself whenever he could. The natural rewards in Bill's life were ignored and he has cognitive control over his drinking. His frontal cortex was unable to suppress the dopaminergic and limbic drives to consume his drug of choice. His habit had become a compulsion and he transitioned into drug abuse—using despite negative consequences.

After a period of a few months, Bill drank every night and thought about drinking during the day. His physical health got worse and he couldn't sleep unless he drank before bed. Some mornings on the weekends he had a drink to calm his nerves. He realized that he probably drinks too much but he thought he could control it and stop whenever he wanted to. Bill's tolerance increased and he became physically dependent on alcohol. Sleep centers in the hypothalamus and brain stem became adapted and he required alcohol to sleep. He used alcohol to suppress the withdrawal symptoms he experienced on some mornings. Bill used denial to defend his behavior.

Bill's poor performance at work was noticed by his supervisors, and Bill's wife told him that he must stop drinking or face the consequences of their separation. Bill slowed down his drinking for a few weeks, but he still drank in secret and minimized the amount he drank. His thinking was impaired throughout the day, he felt unable to find a solution to his problems, and he felt defeated and hopeless. Bill was an alcoholic. He drank despite consequences, he was tolerant and dependent on alcohol, and drank compulsively. If Bill did not stop drinking he would most likely cause significant harm to himself—physically, mentally or legally, or to someone else. There was a strong possibility that Bill would even die if he didn't quit.

Bill's wife, family, and friends all noticed that he had a drinking problem and decided to confront him. They researched local treatment facilities, talked to a couple of experts, and planned a course of recovery for him. They took Bill to a family meeting and expressed their love and support. They asked him to be willing to be assessed by a professional and enter treatment. Bill was acting completely on his motivational and drive systems in his brain. He no longer responded to rational thought and was incapable of suppressing these drives. Bill's family attempted to reach past these self-centered drives and appeal to him on the basis of their love. Bill's denial was met with firm resolve and support. Bill's family had conducted an **intervention**. Bill agreed to be interviewed and assessed by a trained professional at a treatment center. He was subsequently admitted.

Many social stigmas associated with addiction and the judgments placed on these individuals are unnecessary, inappropriate, and may lead to further compulsive behaviors. In our example, Bill responded to the care and support that his family and friends were willing to provide him. He had an honest desire to receive help and was willing to learn about his illness and take responsibility for his recovery.

KEY STEPS IN RECOVERY FROM ADDICTION

For individuals to experience successful recovery from drug and alcohol addiction, they should have a treatment plan that is matched to their individual needs. These depend on factors such as their level of dependence upon the drug, their drug of choice, and their willingness to change (Table 6.2).

The initial medical treatments are highly dependent upon the abused drug. The first step is chemical **detoxification** (detox). The main objective in detox is medical management. Individuals should be treated in a controlled medical setting where their symptoms of drug withdrawal and any other medical conditions can be properly treated. Detox procedures typically last from two to seven days and depend on the overall health of the individual and the drug of choice. During this time, they may be given medications to help them cope with the withdrawal symptoms. For example, heroin users may be given anti-diarrhea medication. Cocaine or amphetamine users may start antidepressant treatment. It is particularly important that individuals who are dependent on alcohol or any other depressants are detoxified in an in-patient hospital setting to protect against the occurrence of life-threatening seizures. The alcohol-dependent brain is accustomed to continuous sedation from alcohol's effect on inhibitory neurotransmitters. When the alcohol is suddenly removed, as in early detox, the brain is easily overexcited and is unable to control its own electrical activity; seizures may occur.

Table 6.2 Neurobiological Correlates of Steps in Drug Addiction and Recovery

BRAIN	BEHAVIOR
Genetic predisposition; environmental stress; drug exposure	May determine rate of progression from initial drug use to abuse
Dopamine surge in nucleus accumbens	Euphoria; drug seeking
Limbic drives supersede cortical control	Abuse progresses into drug dependence and compulsiveness
Internal or external signals force or compel behavior to change	Honest desire for change; "hitting bottom;" sobriety sought
Drug free state; anti-craving medications	Drive cycles broken; recovery starts
Natural rewards are reinforcing	Interests in food, sleep, and family nurturing return
Hypothalamic balance	Sleep cycles and appetite return
Frontal cortex control	Emotional and impulse control
Cognitive development	Contentment in sobriety

Drug craving during the initial detox period can be very intense for certain individuals and is specific for each class of drugs of abuse. **Anti-craving compounds**, discussed in Chapter 7, are used to combat these symptoms. In opiate withdrawal, individuals may be given a substitute opiate and then slowly weaned off the substitute to control their discomfort and cravings. Methadone and LAAM® (levo-alpha-acetyl-methadol) are used successfully in detox and early in-patient rehabilitation programs as substitute opiates. These agents are agonists at opiate receptors in the brain. The binding of these receptors in cells that surround the ventral tegmentum is believed to reduce their cravings. The methadone doses are then tapered in the controlled detox and rehab environments.

The overall general physical and mental health of the individual is addressed in detox settings. Serious diseases or conditions such as high blood pressure, malnourishment, diabetes, and dehydration are treated. Adequate diet and rest are also encouraged. Co-existing mental disorders are addressed and treated in these settings as well. However, completion of the detoxification stage is not enough for individuals to successfully remain drug-free. Individuals who return home to daily living at this stage are extremely vulnerable to relapse. In this stage the brain is very sensitive to stress and environment. If emotional or physical stress is sensed by the brain (particularly the frontal cortex and limbic areas), the chances of relapse are very high. The amygdala and nucleus accumbens respond to sensory stimuli that predict reward and may elicit immediate sensations of drug-craving. In this respect, the brain needs to be free from these triggers as much as possible during this period.

At this point the individual may enter an extended in-patient rehabilitation program. A typical stay at an in-patient facility is between two weeks and six months. A minimum of a three-month stay in these treatment programs has been shown to be very successful for long-term sobriety. During rehabilitation, individuals identify their initial reasons for drug use and the areas of their lives that need work and improvement, and take part in individual and group counseling. They also acknowledge their addictive problems, address and commit to working on their weakness, reach out to others they may have harmed or to those from which they would like support, and commit to continually work on themselves and others struggling with similar problems. It is essential that individuals learn to accept that their addictions are chronic, progressive, and fatal if left untreated.

In Bill's case, he will enter a detox facility, either in a hospital or treatment center, where his physical and mental status will be assessed. His level of alcohol dependence will be determined and treated accordingly. He will be given medications to prevent seizures, multivitamins to protect his brain from any further damage from vitamin deficiencies, and other medications to control his blood pressure, heart rate, and anxiety. His will be discharged within 10 days and enter an in-patient rehab program. Unfortunately, Bill will need to determine which program his health insurance will cover or which one he can afford. During this time period, Bill's neurotransmitter balance will return to normal. His drives for drug-taking will subside and he will regain cortical control over his impulses. A proper balance between limbic and frontal cortical system will continue to improve if he remains drug free and healthy.

Upon release from rehab, Bill can return home or stay in a residential treatment facility such as a **half-way house**, where he can go to work during the day and at night stay in the drug-free, controlled, and supportive environment. The length of stay in these settings typically varies between one month and one year. Upon returning to his family and home, Bill may enroll in a three-month intensive out-patient program (IOP) in the evenings where he will continue to learn stress-management and self-improvement techniques. Bill can use these techniques for relapse prevention by controlling stress, minimizing drug-taking cues, and using other coping mechanisms to deal with his life.

■ **Learn more about the cause of addictive behaviors** Search the Internet for *genetics of alcoholism* or *addiction and stress*.

SUMMARY POINTS

- Having an alcoholic parent or grandparent significantly increases an individual's chances of developing compulsive behaviors, including addiction.

- Critical steps in recovery from addictions include admitting the problem, professional assessment, detoxification, rehabilitation, minimization of drug-associated stimuli and stress, and group and individual therapy.

7 | Addiction Treatments

There are treatments for drug and alcohol addiction, but there are no cures. Group and individual counseling are critical for maintaining sobriety for most individuals. One behavioral treatment strategy involves **cognitive behavioral therapy** (CBT). In CBT, therapists teach their clients to recognize how their thoughts and feelings translate into actions that may threaten their sobriety and abstinence. Clients are taught how to avoid specific situations that may lead to drug use and relapse, how to recognize thoughts that lead to craving, and how to control their emotions in situations that may lead to drug use. The patients analyze their thoughts, plan appropriate actions, and control their impulses. In other words, patients learn how to gain cognitive, cortical control of their drug-seeking urges and drives. CBT takes several months to learn and use successfully. Unfortunately, studies have found that individuals who have suffered cortical damage or have cognitive deficits (such as those from amphetamine or cocaine abuse) struggle with learning and remaining in CBT programs. However, the longer a patient remains in behavioral therapy, the greater their chance of remaining abstinent.

Other experimental techniques have employed the use of incentives as rewards for continued sobriety. Clients are given small prizes and even supportive words of encouragement or praise to remain drug-free. Other studies have examined the use of **vouchers** earned in exchange for drug free urine samples. The vouchers may be exchanged for community goods or services that provide pleasurable alternatives to drug use. Early data from these studies suggest that incentives and vouchers act as positive, non-pharmacologic reinforcement strategies that can be learned by individuals who were once engaged in very impulsive and high-risk behaviors. Future therapies may use additional techniques to teach patience and the value of legal alternatives to drug use.

Learning behavioral control is very difficult for individuals in early recovery. Recent experimental therapies include behavioral training to block the learned associations between drug cues, drug craving, and drug rewards (known as extinction). This type of extinction training in laboratory animals has resulted in increased frontal cortex control of the nucleus accumbens and subsequent drug-seeking behavior. Researchers state that in the future, computer simulation or video games may train the addicted individual that particular environments or cues no longer predict reward or pleasure. However, for most individuals, patience, dedication to long-term goals, and behavioral control are very difficult in early recovery. These patients may benefit from medications as well as behavior therapies.

MEDICATIONS

While cognitive therapies and behavioral strategies are very effective in prevention of relapse and maintenance of abstinence, recent advances have also been made in the development of medications that are used in various stages of recovery. These medications are used for management of early withdrawal symptoms, the treatment of drug craving, and the long-term maintenance of sobriety (Table 7.1).

Table 7.1 Some Medications Used for Addictive Disorders

MEDICATION	BEHAVIORAL EFFECT	MECHANISM OF ACTION
Nicotine replacement preparations	Reduce nicotine withdrawal symptoms (cravings)	Nicotinic receptor agonist; increases synaptic levels of dopamine
Bupropion (Zyban, Wellbutrin)	Reduce nicotine cravings	Dopamine, norepinephrine, and serotonin reuptake blocker
Buprenorphine/ naloxone	Reduce opiate cravings; relapse prevention	Combination of opiate receptor agonist/ antagonist
GVG; D_3 receptor blockers	Reduces cocaine-induced euphoria and drug-seeking behavior	Reduces dopamine surge caused by drugs of abuse
Cocaine antibodies	Prevents drug of abuse from reaching brain	Recognition, binding, and inactivation of drug in blood

Anti-craving Compounds

Anti-craving medications designed to replace the drug of abuse have been used for decades. These medications are used to slowly taper the dose of a drug over time. In this way, withdrawal symptoms are minimized. However, for some preparations of these replacement drugs, the users are left to determine their dosing schedule for themselves. They must then adhere to this schedule during the taper. **Nicotine replacement** devices are used in this manner. Nicotine replacement patches, gum, and inhalers are available on the market without a prescription. As we know, nicotine is a very powerful drug of abuse and is very difficult to quit once dependence has occurred. The individual who uses nicotine replacement preparations must be extremely dedicated to the ultimate goal of abstinence. For these individuals, group and individual therapy are recommended in conjunction with taper regimens.

One of the first anti-craving medications that targeted the neurotransmitters involved with reinforcement and craving was **bupropion** (also known as Zyban® or Wellbutrin®). Bupropion is a relatively weak presynaptic re-uptake blocker of dopamine, norepinephrine, and serotonin in the brain. For these reasons, buproprion was originally marketed as an antidepressant. By slightly increasing the level of dopamine in synapses in dopaminergic reward pathways, craving is reduced in some individuals. Although bupropion is not effective for all smokers, it was the first medication in a new class of anti-craving compounds that involved targeting the dopaminergic reward systems.

More recent medications designed to alter the dopaminergic system include compounds that have been used for other neurological diseases that involve dopaminergic systems. For individuals who are unsuccessful at abstinence from nicotine, a Parkinson's disease medication may provide benefit. Craving from nicotine withdrawal is associated with sharp declines in dopamine in the reward pathways. **Selegiline** has been shown to increase synaptic levels of dopamine because it inhibits the enzyme monoamine oxidase-B (MAO-B). This enzyme is normally present in dopaminergic synapses and is responsible for the metabolism of dopamine following presynaptic release. In early trials, selegiline has been shown to combat nicotine cravings and lead to prolonged abstinence in heavy smokers. Future studies will determine if selegiline has widespread therapeutic potential.

Opiate Addiction Medications

In 2002, the Food and Drug Administration (FDA) approved a combination medication for the treatment of opiate addiction. The medication is a mixture of **buprenorphine** (an opiate receptor agonist) and naloxone (an opiate receptor antagonist). The buprenorphine is believed to bind to opiate receptors and decrease the intense cravings that opiate-addicted individuals experience. The naloxone prevents other opiates of abuse from having effects. This combination therapy has been very successful in the treatment of opiate withdrawals and the prevention of relapse. This combination medication was formerly available only in treatment centers, but is now available for use in the doctor's office setting. A new, longer-lasting preparation of the medication is becoming available, which will require only one dose per month.

Relapse Prevention Medications

Other dopaminergic compounds are currently being investigated as potential agents to decrease the possibility of relapse in recovery. Vigabatrin® (**GVG**) is a GABAergic drug that is used to treat epilepsy. GVG has been shown in laboratory experiments to reduce the dopamine surge caused by cocaine and other stimulants. As a result, animals demonstrate less addictive behavior when pre-treated with GVG. Clinical trials of GVG on humans are underway and have shown promising results. These data suggest that medications that modulate the response of the dopaminergic system to drugs of abuse may be beneficial for the treatment of relapse.

Medications have also been developed to interact directly with dopaminergic receptors in the ventral tegmental reward pathways. The nucleus accumbens and frontal cortex are two areas of the brain that are sensitive to the pleasurable effects of drugs of abuse that possess different receptors for dopamine. Three types of dopamine receptors have been studied in these areas as potential targets for medications (the D_1, D_2, and **D_3 dopamine receptors**). Some laboratory studies have shown that agonists that bind and activate the D_1 and D_2 receptors are too rewarding and pleasurable and would end up being abused as much as cocaine or amphetamine. Yet, blockers or antagonists to these receptors have been shown to cause depression. Antagonists at the D_3 receptor have shown the most promise as potential therapeutic agents. Experimental D_3 receptor blockers reduce the pleasurable effects of cocaine and reduce drug-seeking behaviors during abstinence in laboratory studies. Additional studies have demonstrated similar effects on behaviors induced by heroin and nicotine use. Future experiments will investigate the safety of these compounds for human use.

Future treatments may also include the use of antibodies to inactivate drugs of abuse in the bloodstream before they reach the brain. Current studies are investigating the possibility of synthetic antibodies that catalyze enzymatic reactions when they recognize and attach to molecules of cocaine, methamphetamine, or other drugs of abuse. Future experiments will continue to address the possible development and use of blood detoxification agents in relapse-prevention programs as well as the possibility of immunizing certain populations of individuals against the effects of specific drugs of abuse.

Other medications being investigated as treatments for addictive disorders include other Parkinson's disease agents (which affect dopaminergic transmission and muscle spasticity), antiepileptic and antiseizure medications, and medications used to treat narcolepsy. The research involved with the development of medications to treat addictive disorders is in its infancy. Undoubtedly, future treatment strategies will be highly dependent upon the individual in recovery, their drug(s) of choice, and the presence of any residual brain damage that occurred during their drug use. Perhaps the most successful strategies will employ a combination of medications (anti-craving compounds and receptor blockers) and behavioral therapies (such as individual and group therapy, and 12-step recovery programs) matched to individuals and their treatment expectations.

■ **Learn more about treatments for addictions** Search the Internet for *addiction and behavioral therapies* or *drug addiction treatment medications.*

CONCLUSION

The human brain is susceptible to all drugs of abuse. Our chemical motivational systems are easily hijacked resulting in dysfunctional behavioral control mechanisms. The brain is also sus-

Behavioral Addictions

Several lines of evidence implicate that the same brain areas involved with drug addiction (ventral tegmental dopaminergic system, the nucleus accumbens, the limbic system, and the frontal cortex) are also altered in those with behavioral addictions (such as gambling, sex addictions, and overeating). The classic hallmarks of addictive behaviors (compulsiveness, impulsiveness, tolerance, dependence, and withdrawal) are also present in individuals with behavioral addictions. Chronic gamblers, food addicts, and sex addicts all state that they engage in these behaviors because it makes them feel good (provides a feeling of pleasure) but that it also removes the negative feelings of agitation or tension when the behavior is absent (reduction of withdrawal symptoms). For some individuals, recovery from these compulsive behavioral addictions is very difficult. While it is easy to recognize that we don't need cocaine or methamphetamine to survive, we do need food, for example. Recovery programs modeled after Alcoholics Anonymous are some of the most successful strategies for regaining behavioral control. Certain medications useful in obsessive-compulsive disorders, such as serotonin-type drugs, have also shown beneficial in behavioral control. High risk/high reward behaviors are becoming more commonplace in society today. Gambling on television, on the Internet, and on computer games will undoubtedly lead to new generations of individuals who struggle with behavioral addictions.

ceptible to behavioral addictions that result in compulsions (see "Behavioral Addictions" box). The recent rise in these behaviors is no surprise given that we are exposed to fast-paced technologies (computers, televisions, means of travel, even food preparation) that set the stage for immediate gratification and the resetting of behavioral control thresholds. We possess the material wealth, the means to acquire psychoactive chemicals, and the access to behaviors that can overcome our normal biological drives and control mechanisms. Yet the technological age has also brought us a better understanding of the human brain. It has led to better medications, diagnostic tools, and novel behavioral therapies with which to diagnose and treat addictive disorders. Public recognition of the impact and causes of addiction has led to the acceptance that addiction is a treatable disease. In this regard, the human brain can be considered not only the cause, but the ultimate solution to problem of addiction.

SUMMARY POINTS
- Successful treatment programs include behavioral therapy in which the individual learns to cope with problems without using drugs or alcohol.
- Some therapies incorporate the use of incentives or prizes to encourage drug-free lifestyles in their clients.
- Medications for treating drug addictions include drug-replacement medications, anti-craving compounds, and other dopaminergic drugs.

Glossary

Action potential   Electrical signal that travels down a nerve cell.

Acetylcholine   Neurotransmitter used between cells in the brain and between cells and muscles in the body.

Addiction   Progressive, chronic brain disease characterized by loss of control; drug use despite harm and denial.

Adenosine   Neurotransmitter that normally inhibits norepinephrine release in the brain.

Amnestic   Any drug that causes memory loss.

Amphetamine   Stimulating drug that increases the action of norepinephrine and dopamine and causes alertness.

Amphetamine psychosis   Drug-induced paranoia and suspiciousness resulting from excess dopamine in frontal lobes.

Amygdala   Nuclei located in the temporal lobes of the brain that process emotion and anticipation of drug delivery.

Anandamide   Neurotransmitter involved with pain control whose receptors also bind chemicals in marijuana.

Analgesia   State of decreased pain sensation.

Anesthesia   State of loss of consciousness.

Anti-craving compounds   Medications used to block the craving for drugs during withdrawal.

Antidote   Any drug that blocks another; typically used in medical emergencies.

Aphasia   Loss of language comprehension or production skills.

Arousal   State of behavioral alertness; very awake and attentive.

Behavioral inhibition   Control of emotions and urges to act.

Black-out   Temporary state of drug-induced amnesia.

Brain stem   Brain area above spinal cord that regulates automatic and vital function such as breathing and heart rate.

Buprenorphine   Drug that binds opiate receptors in the brain; used for pain control and treatment of heroin users.

Bupropion   Anti-craving drug that increases dopamine, norepinephrine, and serotonin levels in brain.

Cannabinoid   Any drug that acts on marijuana-like receptors in the brain.

Cerebellum   Area in the back of the brain responsible for muscle balance, coordination, and some forms of learning.

Cerebral cortex   Outer surface of the brain involved with higher intellectual functions such as planning, logic, reasoning, and emotional control.

Cognitive   Mental activities such as thinking and learning.

Cognitive behavioral therapy   Drug counseling that uses thinking and acting to solve problems and change bad behaviors.

Compulsive   Irresistible urge to perform an act repeatedly.

D_3 dopamine receptor   Dopamine receptor in pleasure center and potential target for future medications.

Date-rape drug   Illegal drug that is secretly given to an unsuspecting individual so they won't resist non-consensual sex.

Dependence   State of drug use when individual will become physically sick or emotionally anxious without drug; closely associated with addiction.

Depression   Medical illness characterized by sadness; responds to antidepressant medications.

Dendrite   Part of nerve cell that receives information from other cells.

Detoxification   Earliest stage of recovery from drug addiction that involves elimination of drug from the body.

Disinhibition   Lack of control over emotions by the highest brain centers.

Dopamine   Neurotransmitter involved with feelings of pleasure, drug seeking, and also muscle movement.

Dorsal raphe system   Groups of cells in the base of the brain that produce neurotransmitter serotonin.

Drug Any chemical found outside the body that can change thoughts, feelings, or actions in the user.

Dynorphin Chemical signal in brain that acts to normally suppress pain; shaped like a small protein.

Endorphin Small protein-like brain chemical involved with pain suppression.

Enkephalin Chemical signal in the brain that acts to normally suppress pain; shaped like a small protein.

Fentanyl Very powerful medication used to suppress pain; typically used in hospital setting.

Fight or flight response Behavioral state in which fear has caused activation of hormones and neurotransmitters to prepare for quick action.

Frontal lobe Furthest forward area of the brain behind the forehead responsible for controlling emotions and behaviors.

Gamma-aminobutyric acid (GABA) Neurotransmitter in the brain that suppresses activity of other cells.

GHB Drug that causes rapid sedation and sleepiness.

Glutamate Neurotransmitter in the brain that increases the activity of other cells.

GVG Experimental medication to treat drug craving.

Half-way house Long-term residential facility that houses individuals recovering from drug addiction.

Hallucinogen Drug that causes distortions of senses (such as vision).

Hemisphere One-half of the brain.

Hippocampus Structure located deep inside the sides of the brain.

Homeostasis In multicelled organisms; the capacity for maintaining the internal environment when conditions change.

Hyperthermic Very high body temperature.

Hypothalamus   Brain structure involved with controlling body temperature, eating, drinking, sleep cycles, and emotions.

Inhalant   Vapor or aerosol that contains a drug which is inhaled.

Inhibitory neurotransmitter   A neurotransmitter that prevents or inhibits action potential to be fired by a neuron.

Internalization   Attending to stimuli within the brain instead of stimuli located in outside world.

Interneurons   Small nerve cells located throughout brain that typically decrease the activity of other cells.

Intervention   A strategy or approach by a group that intends to change the actions or behavior of an individual.

Ketamine   Drug typically used in veterinarian practices but can be drug of abuse.

Korsakoff's syndrome   Brain disease in malnourished alcoholics; characterized by poor memory.

Limbic system   Area of the brain responsible for emotions and memory.

Lipophilic   Dissolvable in fat.

Locus ceruleus   Group of nerve cells in the base of brain that produce norepinephrine.

LSD (Lysergic Acid Diethylamide)   Drug that cause distortions of reality.

Marijuana   Drug made from the dried flowers and leaves of the hemp plant. When smoked or eaten, causes intoxication.

MDMA (Ecstasy)   Drug that causes release of serotonin that leads to pleasurable feelings followed by depression.

Mescaline   Drug found in cacti that causes distortions of senses and reality.

Mesolimbic and mesocortical pathways   Neurotransmitter pathways in the brain that deliver dopamine to pleasure centers.

Methamphetamine   Stimulant drug that acts by increasing dopamine and norepinephrine release in brain.

Midbrain   Area in the center of brain that produces neurotransmitters for other parts of the brain.

Monoamine oxidase   Enzyme that breaks down neurotransmitters and some drugs of abuse.

Motor   Brain systems involved with control of muscle movement.

Naloxone   Blocker of pain suppressing drugs; used in medical situations to prevent overdose.

Neuron   Smallest functional unit in brain; nerve cell.

Neuromodulator   Small protein that acts as neurotransmitter to change activity of groups of neurons.

Neuropeptide   Small protein in the brain; usually acts like neurotransmitter.

Neurotransmitter   Chemical signal in the brain; main means of cellular communication.

Nicotine replacement   Medication strategy whereby a nicotine-addicted individual is given smaller and smaller doses of nicotine in gum, skin patch, or inhaler.

Nigrostriatal system   Dopamine system involved with controlling muscle movement; damaged in Parkinson's disease.

Norepinephrine   Neurotransmitter that causes arousal and alertness when released.

Nuclei   Group of cell bodies in the brain.

Nucleus accumbens   Area of the brain that is very sensitive to drugs of abuse; when activated causes pleasure.

Occipital lobe   Area of the back of the brain involved with vision.

Opioid   Drug or chemical that blocks pain signals in the brain.

OxyContin®   Pain medication that is often abused.

Overdose   Emergency medical situation resulting from ingestion of large doses of drug.

Painkiller   Any drug or medication that blocks pain signals.

Parietal lobe   Part of the brain responsible for processing information about sense of touch.

PCP (Phencyclidine)   Drug that causes distortions of reality and feelings of separation from body.

Pons   Area in base of brain responsible for transferring signals between the spinal cord and the brain's higher centers.

Predisposition   Tendency to develop a disease; a susceptibility arising from a hereditary or other factor.

Prefrontal cortex   Area of the brain responsible for planning, decision making, and controlling emotions and drives; implicated in the loss of control associated with addiction.

Psilocybin   Active ingredient in mushrooms that cause distortions of reality.

Psychoactive   Any drug that affects the brain and behavior.

Raves   Large parties of young dancers; can be associated with drug use.

Receptor   Protein on the brain cell surface that recognizes a brain chemical or drug.

Receptor binding   Act of drug or brain chemical binding to a receptor that leads to a change in the activity of a cell.

Recreational or social drug use   Stage of drug taking when a user seeks out drug for effects but is not using in a consistent pattern.

Relapse   Returning to drug/substance use after a period of not using drugs or other substances.

REM sleep   Dream sleep during which rapid eye movement occurs.

Reticular activating system (RAS)   Network of brain cells in base of brain responsible for consciousness, alertness, and reflexes such as sneezing, vomiting, and swallowing.

Re-uptake   Cellular mechanism of inactivation of neurotransmitters in synapse.

Reward   A stimulus that causes pleasure and increases the likelihood that the reward will be sought again.

Rohypnol®   Strong drug that causes sleepiness and forgetfulness; very powerful when mixed with alcohol.

Schizophrenia   Brain disease characterized by irrational thoughts.

Sedative-hypnotic   Drugs that produce sleep or drowsiness—e.g., sleeping pills and tranquilizers.

Selegiline   Medication used for patients with Parkinson's disease that may provide benefit in addiction treatment.

Sensory   Relating to one of five senses (sight, hearing, taste, smell, or touch).

Serotonin   Brain neurotransmitter involved with controlling mood, sleep, and eating.

Soma   Body of nerve cell; processes incoming signals from other neurons; contains nucleus.

SSRIs   Specific serotonin re-uptake inhibitors used for treatment of depression (such as Prozac® and Zoloft®).

Stimulants   Class of drugs characterized by behavioral alertness, wakefulness, and muscular activity.

Stroke   Rupturing or blocking of blood vessel in or around the brain; causes lack of oxygen and possible brain damage.

Sudden cardiac arrhythmias   Fatal skipping of heart beats.

Synapse   Gap between nerve cells; point of integration of information in the brain.

Synergistic   Combined effects of drugs that exceeds the sum of their individual effects.

Temporal lobe   The sides of the brain just behind the ears; involved with hearing and language.

Thalamus   Area deep inside the center of the brain that is responsible for transmitting signal to and from different parts of the brain.

Tolerance   Loss of reduction in the normal response to a drug or other substance, following prolonged use.

Toxicity   Point at which drug dose causes damage.

Tranquilizers Class of drugs that induce sleep and muscle relaxation.

Ventral tegmentum (VTA) Area in the middle of the brain that produces dopamine, which is released into pleasure centers.

Vicodin® Medication used for pain control; becoming more popular as drug of abuse.

Vouchers Prizes or words of praise given to individuals in drug-treatment programs to encourage a drug-free lifestyle.

Withdrawal Unpleasant behavioral and physical state induced by the absence of drug.

Bibliography

American Psychiatric Association. *Diagnostic and Statistical Manual of Mental Disorders, 4ᵗʰ Ed.* Washington, DC: American Psychiatric Association, 2000.

Diaz, J. *How Drugs Influence Behavior: A Neuro-Behavioral Approach.* Upper Saddle River, NJ: Prentice Hall, 1997.

Falkowski, C. *Dangerous Drugs: An Easy to Use Reference for Parents and Professions.* Center City, MN: Hazelden, 2000.

Graham, A. W., et al. *Principles of Addiction Medicine, 3ʳᵈ Ed.* Chevy Chase, MD: American Society of Addiction Medicine, 2003.

Inaba, D. S., and W. E. Cohen. *Upper, Downers, All Arounders, 5ᵗʰ Ed.* Ashland, OR: CNS Publications, Inc.

Julien, R. M. *A Primer of Drug Action.* New York, NY. Henry Holt and Company, 2001.

Kandel, E. R., J. H. Schwartz, and T. M. Jessell. *Principles of Neural Science, 4ᵗʰ Ed.* New York, NY. McGraw Hill, 2000.

National Institute on Drug Abuse. *2003 Monitoring the Future Survey. www.nida.nih.gov/Infofax/HSYouthtrends.html*

Olive, M. *Designer Drugs.* Philadelphia, PA: Chelsea House Publishers, 2004.

Stimmel, B. *The Facts About Drug Use.* Binghamton, NY: Haworth Medical Press, 1993.

Further Reading

Fields, R. *Drugs in Perspective, 5th Ed.* New York, NY: McGraw Hill Publishers, 2004.

Kuhn, C, S Swartzwelder, and W Wilson. *Buzzed: The Straight Facts about the Most Used and Abused Drugs.* New York, NY: W.W. Norton & Company, 1998.

Twerski, A. *The Spiritual Self: Reflections on Recovery and God.* Center City, MN: Hazelden, 2000.

■ Websites

National Institute on Alcohol Abuse and Alcoholism.
  www.niaaa.nih.gov

National Institute on Drug Abuse.
  www.nida.nih.gov

Substance Abuse and Mental Health Services Administration.
  www.health.org

National Institute on Drug Abuse, website designed specifically for
  teenagers.
  http://teens.drugabuse.gov/

Index

Acetylcholine, 48, 88
Action potential, 9, 23, 88
Addiction, cycle of
    early behavior, 70–75
    environment, 67, 69–70, 76
    heredity and genetics, 66–67,
        69, 72, 76, 78
    progression, 71–75
    recovery steps, 72, 75–87
Addiction, drug, 1, 88
    and the brain, 5–36, 41,
        49, 86
    economic cost, 2
    signs and symptoms, 3–4, 32
    statistics, 2–3
    and stress, 68–69, 72–73,
        78
    treatment, 4
Adenosine, 46, 88
Alcohol addiction, 1, 44
    economic cost, 2
    effects of addiction, 5, 7, 24–25,
        29–30, 36, 52–54, 58,
        68–69, 72
    and genetics, 5, 67, 69, 71, 75,
        78
    and other drugs, 56
    poisoning and overdoses,
        10, 53, 91
    signs and symptoms, 3, 33, 53
    tolerance and dependence,
        73–75
    treatment, 4, 54, 74–87
    use, 3
    withdrawal symptoms, 52–53,
        74–75
Amnestic properties, 88
    of depressants, 25
Amphetamine
    abuse effects, 7, 21, 29–32,
        36–42, 44, 50, 80, 84
    and hyperactivity disorders, 14
    overdose, 16, 42

psychosis, 40, 88
use of, 2–3
withdrawal, 75–76
Amygdala
    functions, 6, 88
    and reward pathway, 33, 35, 77
    steroid abuse in, 7
    targets of addiction, 7, 32
Analgesia, 50, 59, 88
Anandamide, 64–65, 88
Anesthesia, 50, 58, 88
Anti-craving compounds
    and recovery, 76–77, 82–83, 85,
        87–89
Antidote, 56, 88
Aphasia, 88
    types, 16
Arousal, 21, 88

Barbiturates
    effects of addiction, 24
    overdose, 10
Behavior
    and addiction, 36, 59, 67, 72–75,
        79, 86
    early, 70
    and inhalants, 58
    inhibition, 13, 41, 56, 88
    and loss of control, 15, 32,
        34–35, 70, 78, 87
    motivation, 26, 45
    risky, 32
    and stimulant abuse, 38, 40–41,
        45
    therapies, 80–81, 85, 87
Benzodiazepines, 55
Binge drinking, 10
Black-outs. 7, 25, 42, 54, 73, 88
Brain
    destructive powers of, 1
    disease and injury, 1, 4–5, 34,
        46, 53, 71, 78, 88, 91
    functions, 1, 6–12, 22–24, 30,
        49, 52

REM sleep, 19, 93
Reticular activating system
    (RAS), 93
    functions, 8–9
Reward, 93
    and addictive behavior, 26–29,
        31–35, 49, 56, 68, 72, 76–77,
        81, 83–84
Rohypnol®, 93
    effects of addiction, 24, 56–57
    overdose, 56–57

Schizophrenia, 14, 50, 70, 93
    symptoms, 40
Sedative-hypnotics, 94
    dependence and addiction, 55
    effects on brain processes,
        55–57, 65
    overdose, 10, 56
    types, 55
Selegiline, 83, 94
Sensory, 94
    information, 6–7, 12
    stimuli, 26
Serotonin, 94
    functions, 19–21, 23, 89–90
    production, 21, 92
    re-uptake, 20, 43, 82–83, 94–95
    targets of addiction, 19–21, 35,
        43, 45–46, 49–50, 59, 73
Serotonin reuptake inhibitors. See
    SSRIs
Sleeping pills, 24
Spinal cord
    structures of, 8–9, 18–19, 22,
        88, 93
SSRIs (Serotonin reuptake
    inhibitors), 20, 94
Steroids
    effects of abuse, 7
    use, 2
Stimulants, 94

abuse effects, 21, 36–48, 59
    stereotypical behaviors, 45
Striatum
    and movement, 23
    targets of addiction, 19
Stroke, 94
    deficits, 16
    drug causes of, 16
Substantia nigra
    structures, 22–24, 62
Sudden cardiac arrhythmias, 59, 94
Synapse, 31, 94
    functions, 8–9, 17–18, 21, 25
    targets for addiction, 39, 51
Synergistic properties, 94
    of depressants, 25

Temporal lobe, 12, 94
    functions, 13, 16, 32, 88
Thalamus, 94
    functions, 6, 53
THC. See Marijuana
Tobacco
    use, 3, 47
Tolerance, 3, 31, 86, 94
    on depressants, 56
    on stimulants, 46–48
Toxicity, 94
Tranquilizers, 2, 94

Ventral tegmentum
    and the addictive properties of
        drugs, 22–23, 28–29, 31, 35,
        67, 69, 86
    and craving and pleasure,
        28–29, 35, 76, 84, 94
    and motivation, 34
Vicodin®, 2, 59, 95
Vouchers, 81, 95

Withdrawal, 5, 48, 86, 95
    symptoms, 4, 32, 75–77, 81–82

About the Author

James D. Stoehr, originally from Pittsburgh, Pennsylvania, received his B.S. in Biology from the University of Pittsburgh at Johnstown in 1987 and his Ph.D. in Physiology from Dartmouth Medical School in 1993. He was a National Institute of Mental Health Postdoctorate Fellow in the Division of Neural Systems, Memory, and Aging at the University of Arizona until 1996 when he joined the faculty of Midwestern University in Glendale, Arizona. He currently teaches neuroscience and physiology and supervises student research projects as a professor in the Colleges of Medicine and Health Sciences.

Dr. Stoehr is the author of publications in the fields of addiction medicine, neurobiology of memory, psychopharmacology, and health professions education. He recently completed a five-year grant from the White House Office of National Drug Control Policy that funded his teaching of the neurobiology of addiction to more than 15,000 high school teenagers in the greater Phoenix area.

Picture Credits